SpringerBriefs in Law

SpringerBriefs present concise summaries of cutting-edge research and practical applications across a wide spectrum of fields. Featuring compact volumes of 50 to 125 pages, the series covers a range of content from professional to academic. Typical topics might include:

- A timely report of state-of-the art analytical techniques
- A bridge between new research results, as published in journal articles, and a contextual literature review
- A snapshot of a hot or emerging topic
- A presentation of core concepts that students must understand in order to make independent contributions

SpringerBriefs in Law showcase emerging theory, empirical research, and practical application in Law from a global author community. SpringerBriefs are characterized by fast, global electronic dissemination, standard publishing contracts, standardized manuscript preparation and formatting guidelines, and expedited production schedules.

Alexandra Juster
Editor

Legal Drafts in Anthropocene Literature

Springer

Editor
Alexandra Juster
University of Innsbruck
Innsbruck, Austria

ISSN 2192-855X ISSN 2192-8568 (electronic)
SpringerBriefs in Law
ISBN 978-3-032-27282-9 ISBN 978-3-032-27283-6 (eBook)
https://doi.org/10.1007/978-3-032-27283-6

This Springer imprint is published by the registered company Springer Nature Switzerland AG
The registered company address is: Gewerbestrasse 11, 6330 Cham, Switzerland

Contents

About the Editor and Contributors

About the Editor

Alexandra Juster is a senior postdoctoral researcher and a habilitation candidate (a qualification required for a professorship in German-speaking countries). She currently leads an interdisciplinary research project in law and literature, funded by the Austrian FWF, at the Institute of Comparative Literature at the University of Innsbruck in Austria. She is a lawyer admitted to the French and Italian bars and holds a PhD in German modern literature. Fields of investigation: Modern literature and interdisciplinary fields at the intersection of literature, law, philosophy, and society, including the Anthropocene, exile, migration, memory, gender, and violence.

About the Contributors

Matthew H. Birkhold is Associate Professor of German at the Ohio State University and faculty Director of the Environmental Humanities minor. He is a scholar of law, culture, and the humanities, with an emphasis on German literature from 1750 to 1945, environmental humanities, intellectual property, and Indigenous studies. His main publications include *Characters before Copyright* (2019), *Chasing Icebergs* (2023), and *Metronome* (2025). He is also an enthusiastic teacher and advisor. His book *Chasing Icebergs* (2023) investigates the world of iceberg harvesting to learn if the frozen freshwater mountains could be a solution to the global water crisis. Interweaving cultural history, personal interviews, and law, it identifies the social, philosophical, legal, and environmental hurdles we must clear to equitably make use of this untapped resource.

Amitabh Vikram Dwivedi is the Dean of the Faculty of Humanities & Social Sciences at Shri Mata Vaishno Devi University, India. He is a linguistic anthropologist and cultural researcher whose work is defined by large, collaborative projects that document languages, revitalize marginal cultures, and map heritage practices.

He co-directed the Indian Council of Social Science Research project "A Comprehensive Study of Culture, Philosophy, Literature and Language of Jammu & Kashmir" (2018–2021), a multi-year effort combining field linguistics with regional cultural mapping. Beyond this flagship grant, Dwivedi has contributed to a wide slate of research and reference projects with international press(es).

Justine Scarlaken is a researcher and lecturer in contemporary literature at the University of Oviedo, Spain, specializing in ecopoetics, Pacific literatures, and theoretical fiction. Her research explores the intersections between literature, law, and legal innovation, with particular attention to feminist materialist and decolonial approaches. She has lived in New Zealand, an experience that deeply informs her work on Pacific Indigenous literatures and Māori sovereignty issues. Her recent publications examine how contemporary literature engages with legal and environmental concerns, as well as narrative strategies in texts addressing systemic violence.

Introduction

Alexandra Juster

This special edition "Legal Drafts in Anthropocene Literature" is based on the idea that the increasing urgency of the climate crisis, whose effects are becoming ever more visible, is inspiring a wealth of novels and writings about the consequences of the Anthropocene. According to Gabriele Dürbeck, the term 'Anthropocene', coined by Paul Crutzen and Eugene Stoermer, refers to "a new geological epoch in which humanity exerts a dominant geophysical influence over the Earth system, thereby assuming responsibility for the planet's future. It also calls for a redefinition of humanity's position in relation to nature and the cosmos, as well as as the responsible use of limited natural resources" (my translation).[1] Bruno Latour strongly emphasised the need to reconsider the human relationship with nature and the non-human, supporting the idea of demolishing the barrier between 'culture and nature'. According to this vision, the human and non-human interact in a common system—Gaia—where no distinction is made between human and non-human actants. The question of responsibility for harm caused to nature, biodiversity and the climate raises legal issues. Literature reflects society and its debates, addressing major issues such as the current, critical escalation of the climate crisis caused by human activity on Earth and the overexploitation of its resources. The literary fictional space allows the human imagination to flourish almost boundlessly, whereas law is bound by its pragmatic aim of solving conflicts and contradictions within society as efficiently as possible. Law must obey pre-established rules of procedure, interpretation and application to avoid arbitrariness, whereas literature has no specific directives to follow. This freedom of thought and experimentation in literature can benefit new legal developments, as literature often anticipates legal needs or identifies legal

[1] Dürbeck (2018a), p. 11.

A. Juster (✉)
University of Innsbruck, Innsbruck, Austria
e-mail: Alexandra.Juster@uibk.ac.at

A. Juster (ed.), *Legal Drafts in Anthropocene Literature*, SpringerBriefs in Law,
https://doi.org/10.1007/978-3-032-27283-6_1

gaps or inadequacies in response to new situations. Such literary sources can inform later legal reflections and amendments required in response to new challenges and threats, such as the devastating consequences of human impact in the current Anthropocene era. Considering these new threats and dangers, authors are envisaging a variety of dystopian, utopian, and hybrid scenarios, some of which highlight legal shortcomings and inadequacies, while others propose legal innovations. As Heinz Müller-Dietz emphasises, literature anticipates social developments and needs that the law only recognises later, stepping behind literary visionaries. Apart from times of radical epochal change or revolutionary upheaval, the law usually lags social developments due to its traditionally conservative character, processing changes late (often too late). This 'cultural lag', or the delay of the law, contrasts with literature's more seismographic character, which picks up on social change processes earlier and more quickly, if not playing a pioneering role.[2] Peter Häberle also attributes a pioneering role to literature in recognising the legal needs of society. This is because it provides the 'material' from which the law and lawyers in an open society can derive inspiration, as well as 'values' in the short, medium and long term.[3] According to Häberle, the "amateurish pre-formulation of reform wishes and necessities, of new human needs and hardships, of hopes and desires" is reason enough "to approach literature and writers".[4] In this sense, this volume attempts to highlight literature's pioneering role as a source of inspiration for later legal drafting in the field of Anthropocene debates. The concept of the Anthropocene is therefore central to this volume and merits further explanation.

It is beyond doubt that there has been a sharp acceleration in the damaging effects of human activities on the Earth system since at least the Second World War, and certainly since the fall of the Berlin Wall in 1989. It was precisely this alarming observation that prompted the atmospheric chemist Paul Crutzen and the biologist Eugene Stoermer to declare the start of the Anthropocene epoch.

> The expansion of mankind, both in numbers and per capita exploitation of Earth's resources has been astounding (5). To give a few examples: During the past 3 centuries human population increased tenfold to 6000 million, accompanied e.g. by a growth in cattle population to 1400 million (6) (about one cow per average size family). Urbanisation has even increased tenfold in the past century. In a few generations mankind is exhausting the fossil fuels that were generated over several hundred million years. The release of SO2, globally about 160 Tg/year to the atmosphere by coal and oil burning, is at least two times larger than the sum of all natural emissions, occurring mainly as marine dimethyl-sulfide from the oceans (7); from Vitousek et al. (8) we learn that 30–50% of the land surface has been transformed by human action; more nitrogen is now fixed synthetically and applied as fertilizers in agriculture than fixed naturally in all terrestrial ecosystems; the escape into the atmosphere of NO from fossil fuel and biomass combustion likewise is larger than the natural inputs, giving rise to photochemical ozone ("smog") formation in extensive regions of the world; more than half of all accessible fresh water is used by mankind; human activity has increased the species extinction rate by thousand to ten thousand fold in the tropical rain forests (9) and

[2] Cf. Müller-Dietz (1990), p. 21.

[3] Cf. Häberle (1983), p. 98.

[4] Ibid., p. 100.

> several climatically important "greenhouse" gases have substantially increased in the atmosphere: CO2 by more than 30% and CH4 by even more than 100%. Furthermore, mankind releases many toxic substances in the environment and even some, the chlorofluorocarbon gases, which are not toxic at all, but which nevertheless have led to the Antarctic 'ozone hole' and which would have destroyed much of the ozone layer if no international regulatory measures to end their production had been taken. Coastal wetlands are also affected by humans, having resulted in the loss of 50% of the world's mangroves. Finally, mechanized human predation ("fisheries") removes more than 25% of the primary production of the oceans in the upwelling regions and 35% in the temperate continental shelf regions (10). Anthropogenic effects are also well illustrated by the history of biotic communities that leave remains in lake sediments. The effects documented include modification of the geochemical cycle in large freshwater systems and occur in systems remote from primary sources (11–13). Considering these and many other major and still growing impacts of human activities on earth and atmosphere, and at all, including global, scales, it seems to us more than appropriate to emphasize the central role of mankind in geology and ecology by proposing to use the term 'anthropocene' for the current geological epoch.[5]

Crutzen and Störmer denounce the impact of human activities on the geology and ecological balance of the planet. These effects are attributable to the rapid increase in the world's population, urbanisation, agricultural practices and the exploitation of natural resources through mechanical and chemical processes. This leads not only to the destruction of soil, water, flora and fauna, but also to the release of harmful gases such as SO_2 and CO_2 into the atmosphere. The two researchers date the beginning of the Anthropocene epoch to the Industrial Revolution and the invention of the steam engine by James Watt. Others date it further back, to the colonisation of North and South America in the early seventeenth century (Lewis/Maslin). Another suggestion refers to the dawn of the nuclear age (Zalasiewicz).[6] Bruno Latour highlights the onset of significant technological acceleration following the Second World War,[7] which has experienced further acceleration since the fall of the Berlin Wall.[8] It should be noted that the recognition of the Anthropocene as a new geological epoch is currently under debate from a geological perspective. Indeed, in March 2024, the International Union of Geological Sciences (IUGS) voted against recognising the Anthropocene as a geological epoch. In their view, it should be understood as an 'event' at most, but not as a geological epoch.[9] However, what remains undisputed is the fundamental observation that the environmentally damaging effects of human activity on the Earth's ecosystem are accelerating rapidly and must now be urgently addressed.[10]

---

[5] Crutzen and Stoermer (2000), pp. 17–18.

[6] Cf. Dürbeck (2018b), pp. 4–5; Zalasiewicz et al. (2024).

[7] Cf. Hüpkes (2020), pp. 4–5.

The 'Great Acceleration' is the term used to describe the dramatic increase in human impact on the Earth's systems since the 1950s.

[8] Cf. Arte (2021); Steffen et al. (2015).

[9] Cf. IUGS (2024).

[10] As early as 1873, Antonio Stoppani recognised the impact of humans as a telluric force, coining the term 'Anthropozoic Era' (Stoppani 1873, pp. 327, 364, 384, 393). In 1926, the Russian geologist V. I. Vernadsky also noted the growing influence of human activities on the environment

The concept of the Anthropocene implies a call to redefine humanity's position in relation to nature and the cosmos, as well as a responsibility to use limited natural resources sustainably.[11]

The concept of the Anthropocene is not only the subject of critical considerations in the scientific field; it has also been the focus of intense attention in literature and the humanities for several years now, extending beyond the natural sciences. Literature deals with observable and future anthropogenic consequences,[12] often presenting scientific findings in a way that is understandable to laypeople.[13] A particular challenge lies in narrating something that is difficult to describe in spatial, phenomenological, and temporal terms.[14] According to Jochen Ostheimer,

> to gain acceptance, understanding and approval, the idea of the Anthropocene needs to be communicated. Narratives are an effective way of explaining complex issues to different target groups, highlighting the urgency of an issue and motivating people to act. Narratives about the Anthropocene provide a means for modern society to reflect on the consequences of its actions on its own structure and self-image (my translation).[15]

This reflexivity is addressed in contemporary literature through a variety of narrative forms, including cli-fi novels, short stories, climate-critical texts, plays and poems. According to Sylvie Mayer, cli-fi novels use fiction to demonstrate to readers the causes and consequences of climate change. In this sense,

> they employ the realm of fiction as an experimental field to address the tangible experience of anthropogenic climate change, its causes, and its current and potential future consequences. In creating fictional worlds, climate change novels draw on a wide range of cultural knowledge. Through their content and design, these novels can engage readers intellectually, emotionally and affectively (my translation).[16]

According to Axel Goodbody and Adeline Johns-Putra, the phenomenon of 'cli-fi' literature emerged in the 2010s.[17] Gregers Andersen dates the beginning of research into climate fiction to Ursula Heise's 2008 work Sense of Place and Sense of Planet, in which she explicitly refers to works dealing with human-induced climate change in her concluding remarks.[18] Goodbody provides the following definition of climate fiction novels:

(Vernadsky 1998). As early as 1979, Gordon MacDonald wrote a report for the US Environmental Protection Agency warning of the alarming rise in CO_2 emissions due to fossil fuel combustion (MacDonald et al. 1979, p. i).

[11] Cf. Dürbeck (2018a), p. 11; see also: Latour (2015), pp. 133–135; Steffen et al. (2007), pp. 614–621; Steffen et al. (2015), p. 94; Crutzen (2002), pp. 23–24; Crutzen (2019); Crutzen and Steffen (2003); Lovelock (2016); Sloterdijk (2015), pp. 25–44; Chakrabarty (2018), pp. 5–32; Edwards (2015); Nesselhauf (2020), pp. 1–6; Stengers (2016), pp. 134–144).

[12] Cf. Böschen and Viehöver (2012), p. 304.

[13] Cf. Viehöver (2011).

[14] Cf. Ghosh (2017).

[15] Ostheimer (2020), pp. 43–44.

[16] Mayer (2015).

[17] Cf. Goodbody and Johns-Putra (2019), p. 230; cf. Glass (2013).

[18] Cf. Andersen (2020), p. 8; Heise (2008), pp. 205–210.

> In the absence of a precise definition, cli-fi is best understood as a specific genre of cultural works dealing with human-induced climate change. These works explore the phenomenon in terms of both setting and psychological and social issues, combining fictional plots with meteorological facts, speculations about the future and reflections on the relationship between humans and nature. These works have open boundaries to a larger archive of related pieces, sometimes drawing on them to portray and describe the climate crisis (my translation).[19]

Examples of climate novels from the English-speaking world include Barbara Kingsolver's *Flight Behaviour* (2013), Robert Edric's *Salvage* (2010), Ian McEwan's *Sola*r (2011), Emmi Itäranta's *Memory of Water* (2014), Kim Stanley Robinson's *New York 2140* (2018) and *The Ministry for the Futu*re (2020), Saci Lloyd's *Carbon Diaries 2015* (2009), and Paolo Bacigalupi's *Water Knife* (2016). The climate novel has also emerged in the German literary scene with works such as Ilija Trojanow's *EisTau* (2011) and Sven Böttcher's *Prophezeiung* (2011). More recently, Gabriele Kiefer's *Der Platz der Engel* (2019) and Heiko Tschischwitz's *Die Welt kippt* (2022) were published. Scandinavia also has a strong climate fiction scene, with notable works including Maja Lunde's *The History of Be*es (2018a), *The History of Water* (2018b), *The Last of Their Kind* (2020) and *The Dream of a Tree* (2023), as well as Jens Liljestrand's *The Beginning of Tomorrow* (2022). In the United Kingdom, John Ironmonger is a leading figure in this trend, having published *The Whale and the End of the Wor*ld (2019), *The Year of the Dugong* (2021), and *The Wager and the Bear* (2023). In France, Gaspar Koenig's *Humus* (2023) and Camille de *Toledo's Le fleuve qui voulait écrire: Les auditions du parlement de Loire* (2021), explore the relationship between humans and nature.

Fictional characters in climate literature can range from realistic to fantastical.[20] Claudine Jacquenod-Desforges[21] describes science fiction as a special form of fiction that falls between fiction and fantasy, in that it is considered unrealistic at the time of writing yet can nevertheless be explained rationally. Hans Esselborn defines science fiction as "the coherent representation of a different world that could be possible in the future or under different material conditions".[22] These thought experiments in science fiction can mostly be assigned to three thematic groups: the technologically and scientifically possible future; the discovery of new worlds; and the relationship between humans and the universe.[23] By creating a deliberate cognitive distance between reality and narrative, science fiction transports readers to another world, which may be wonderful, hyper-technological, or apocalyptic. In the latter case, science fiction becomes an end-time scenario, a feature typical of the collapsology movement.[24] Unlike the discourse of sustainable thinking and action, which simultaneously shows possible ways out of the dilemma, collapsological

[19] Goodbody and Johns-Putra (2018), pp. 1–2.

[20] Cf. Klauk and Köppe (2014); Zipfel (2014); Bareis (2014); Searle (1975); Eco (1994).

[21] Cf. Jacquenod-Desforges (2022), p. 144.

[22] Esselborn (2019), p. 49.

[23] Cf. Ibid., p. 76.

[24] Cf. Jacquenod-Desforges (2022), p. 149.

discourse announces the imminent, inevitable collapse of the world. Yves Cochet sees the imminent collapse of the globalised world in the fact that the basic needs of the world's population (water, food, housing, clothing, energy, mobility and security) can no longer be met, which he believes will lead to the decline of the entire world system.[25] In fantastic climate novels, on the other hand, the impossible breaks into reality.[26] According to Moritz Baßler, "Fantasy worlds [...] are simulations, yes, but not of aspects of our world. Rather, they attempt to construct a new, attractive, independent and particularly habitable world—a commodity for which there is apparently considerable demand in our time".[27]

The diversity of fictional climate novels is further enriched by a wide variety of realistic narratives, reports and analyses that increasingly draw on objective scientific findings. Christian Klein and Matías Martínez address this issue by examining the narrative form of reality storytelling as 'the fundamental form of our access to reality".[28] By this, they mean references within the diegesis to facts that exist outside it. They distinguish between descriptive, normative, and predictive narratives of reality.[29] According to Klein and Martínez, the term 'narrative' refers to the "linguistic representation of an event, i.e. a temporally organised sequence of events",[30] the connections of which create meaning.[31] These connections can, under certain circumstances, be classified into specific overarching narratives, such as "problem narratives of anthropogenic global climate change and its negative effects on humans and the environment".[32] In the context of climate change and the Anthropocene, Thomas Klein argues that narrative is a meaningful technique for highlighting impending developments or possibilities for implementing a new social utopia.[33] Harald Welzer and Klaus Wiegandt view narrative as a means of inspiring people to modify their habits and ways of thinking.[34]

Importantly, Gabriele Dürbeck summarises the features generally found in anthropogenic narratives as follows: "understanding humanity as a geophysical force; having a deep temporal dimension; taking a planetary perspective on the global environmental crisis; assuming the inseparability of nature and culture; and deriving from this an ethical responsibility of humans for the Earth system".[35] According to Dürbeck, the anthropogenic narrative can be divided into five

[25] Cf. Cochet (2019), p. 23.

[26] Cf. Esselborn (2019), p. 47.

[27] Baßler (2013), p. 44; cf. Kindt (2011), p. 49; Todorov (1970), pp. 28–43.

[28] Klein and Martínez (2009), p. 1; Römer (2012), p. 104.

[29] Cf. Ibid., p. 6.

[30] Ibid.

[31] Cf. Klein (2013), p. 18.

[32] Viehöver (2012), pp. 173–215, cit. in Böschen and Viehöver (2012), p. 304.

[33] Cf. Klein (2020), p. 40.

[34] Cf. Welzer and Wiegandt (2011), p. 9.

[35] Cf. Dürbeck (2018a), p. 13.

categories: the hopeless apocalypse, in which human action comes too late;[36] the great transformation, which considers it possible to avert catastrophe through swift action;[37] the salvation of the Earth through technology;[38] the question of guilt and cause;[39] and the repositioning of humans in the Gaia hypothesis.[40] In view of the global challenge of the Anthropocene, to which Amitav Ghosh refers in *The Great Derangement: Climate Change as the Unthinkable* (2016), "new narratives for the constitution and communication of meaning are necessary".[41] *Examples of such narratives include Grit Kalies' Raumzeit (*2019*), Andri S. Magnason's On Time and Water* (2021), and Aurélien Barrau's *L'Hypothèse K.* (2023).

Many fictional climate novels and real-narrative texts not only raise legal issues and gaps, but also convey ideas, suggestions and drafts for possible new legal frameworks explicitly or implicitly. In *On Time and Water*, for example, the Icelandic writer Andri Snær Magnason proposes a concept for a new legal framework. Similarly, when Gabriele Kiefer introduces the energy pass in her novel *Platz der Engel*, it provides inspiration for new legal approaches.[42] In addition to explicit suggestions, implicit drafts of legal reforms can also be adopted. In *Die Welt kippt*, for instance, Heiko von Tschischwitz suggests that capitalism could be compelled by mandatory legal provisions to address environmental issues.[43] Conversely, Bruno Latour insists on ending the dialectic between humans as subjects and the Earth as an object.[44] Such a new perspective encourages reflection on the status of the 'legal subject', or more generally, on a state of emergency due to the urgency of the situation. In *L'Hypothèse K.*, French astrophysicist Aurélien Barrau prioritises environmental catastrophe as a research subject, suggesting new research responsibilities. The list of literary treatments of legal issues relating to the Anthropocene is therefore long.

An initial inventory of legal proposals and drafts shows that the texts criticise the inadequacy, or even the complete absence, of legal instruments capable of effectively countering the climate crisis. They consider how such a global phenomenon as the Anthropocene can be defined legally to hold individuals or groups accountable for environmental damage. They address the difficulty of determining damage and proving causality between perpetrators and the damage caused. They also consider whether and how legal action and proceedings could force harmful actors to take responsibility for climate change. The texts discuss terms such as ecocide, terracide and geocide, as well as the concept of responsibility in relation to the

[36] Cf. Sloterdijk (2015); Malkmus (2015); Oreskes et al. (2014); Colebrook (2014).

[37] Cf. Crutzen and Steffen (2021); Steffen (2007); Schwägerl (2012).

[38] Cf. Steffen (2007); Crutzen (2006); Lynch (2007); Hamilton (2016).

[39] Cf. Sloterdijk (2015); Chakrabarty (2018).

[40] Cf. Lovelock (2016); Latour (2015); Stengers (2016), cit. in Dürbeck (2018a), p. 13.

[41] Dürbeck (2018b), p. 7.

[42] Cf. Kiefer (2019), p. 31.

[43] Cf. Von Tschischwitz (2022), p. 54.

[44] Cf. Latour (2015), p. 36.

moral and ethical obligations of individuals, groups, states and the community as a whole. Other considerations focus on legal issues, such as granting nature legal entity or even legal personality status. Concerns are raised about mass violence and brutalisation, and whether these can be countered by legal means. New legal projects and solutions are being drafted. The texts denounce the unfair distribution of responsibility for climate change between those who are responsible for it and those who are affected by it, and between rich and poor countries, as well as between post-colonial and Western countries. All the texts grapple with the difficulty of legal systems meeting this new, boundless challenge of climate change.

This special edition, "Legal Drafts in Anthropocene Literature", brings together five contributions that highlight the difficulties involved in addressing the question of how law should respond to the current climate crisis, and what form this response could take, through the example of different literary texts. The following chapters address these questions in different ways and formats, often implicitly, and range from climate novels to poems.

In "The Principle of Responsibility in Climate Novels: An Encounter Between Literature and Law", **Alexandra Juster** considers the possibility of holding individuals and/or collectives accountable for climate damage. In contrast, in "Jean Giono's The Man Who Planted Trees: Critical Nature Writing, Enlivement, and Humans as Trustees of Nature", she considers the relationship between humans and nature in terms of legal status (i.e. legal subject or legal object) and shows the idea of humans as nature's caretakers.

Justine Scarlaken analyses in her contribution "From Beaver Alliances to River Parliaments: New Legal Narratives and Interspecies Representation in Contemporary French Literature (2019–2025)" legal experiments in contemporary French literature in which rivers become legal entities.

In "I Am the Cold / I Am the Melt": Poetic Testimony and the Right to Be Cold in Jessie Kleemann's *Arkhticós Dolorôs* (2019)" **Matthew H. Birkhold** analyses how Jessie Kleemann's Arkhticós Dolorôs can be read as a speculative lawsuit against ice melt.

In conclusion of this special edition, **Amitabh Vikram Dwivedi** shows in his contribution "Ecocide as Speech Act: How Anthropocene Narratives Perform New Crimes into Legal Thinkability", how the legal crime of ecocide becomes imaginable through narrative acts.

In her chapter "The Principle of Responsibility in Climate Novels: An Encounter Between Literature and Law", Alexandra Juster demonstrates literature's ability to observe and record social contexts, needs, crises, fears, desires, and hopes. While law regulates situations and circumstances at a specific point in history, literature highlights legal inconsistencies, shortcomings and gaps, and anticipates legal needs. Building on this premise, the chapter elaborates on the legally relevant discourse related to the concept of responsibility, with a particular focus on literary discourse concerning individual and collective responsibility in association with the climate crisis, as depicted in *Platz der Engel* (2019) by Gabriele Kiefer, *Der Eisbär und die Hoffnung auf Morgen* (2024) by John Ironmonger, and *Humus* (2024) by Gaspard Koenig.

Juster's chapter first addresses the concept of responsibility from legal and ethical perspectives. Legally speaking, responsibility presupposes a person of sound mind, a free act, and a causal connection between the act and its consequences. In the Anthropocene era, however, this concept takes on a new dimension: responsibility now encompasses the individual and collective obligation to protect the planet's natural resources. International agreements such as the 2015 Paris Climate Agreement, national constitutional reforms, and case law are increasingly taking this responsibility into account, cautiously opening to the idea of holding states and corporations accountable.

The literary analysis illustrates this discourse on responsibility using three novels. In Gabriele Kiefer's *Platz der Engel* (Place of Angels), the energy pass is used to develop a model for measuring and regulating individual CO_2 emissions, offering a reflection on the difficulty of measuring personal responsibility on a global scale. Gaspar Koenig, on the other hand, exposes the irresponsibility of capitalist profit logic in *Humus*, highlighting that collective consumer behaviour could force economic actors to act ethically. Finally, in *Der Eisbär und die Hoffnung auf Morgen* (*The Wager and the Bear*), John Ironmonger focuses on the responsibility of politicians: those who are incapable of action due to cowardice or self-interest become accomplices to a structural catastrophe.

The chapter's central insight can be summarised as follows: legal regulations alone cannot stop the climate catastrophe. Rather, a fundamental ethical attitude is needed that encompasses all actors—both individuals and collectives. In this sense, all three novels point to the need for a global culture of responsibility that transcends national borders, cultural differences, and ideological differences. Only through the interaction of legal instruments and a globally shared ethical responsibility can the Anthropocene be effectively addressed.

Alexandra Juster highlights in her chapter "Jean Giono's The Man Who Planted Trees: Critical Nature Writing, Enlivement, and Humans as Trustees of Nature" the highly seismographic nature of literature. Seventy years ahead of its time, it anticipates current legal debates on the relationship between nature and culture. As early as 1953, Jean Giono's eco-critical short story "The Man Who Planted Trees" anticipated current Anthropocene debates about man-made causes of nature's destruction, as well as the interactions and interrelationships between nature and culture. Giono questions the anthropocentric worldview of Western society and attempts to develop a biocentric counter-model, which bears a striking resemblance to indigenous concepts of law and worldviews, as reflected in the Ecuadorian constitution of 2008.

From Giono's short emerges an anticipated vision of nature as a legal subject. While Western legal systems traditionally grant legal subjectivity only to humans, treating nature as an exploitable object, indigenous cultures, and increasingly progressive constitutions such as Ecuador's and Chile's constitution, recognise nature as an independent legal subject. Concepts such as *Pachamama* and *sumak kawsay* formulate a biocentric understanding of humans and nature as equal parts of a whole—a view that Western anthropocentrism has systematically denied since the time of Descartes.

The landscape encountered by the wanderer is ruined—a ‘fractal structure’ of devastated nature and abandoned villages, where misery and disease reign supreme. The central character, Elzéard Bouffier, responds not with despair, but with systemic patience: he plants trees for decades without asking who owns the land. His actions bring about ‘enlivement’, i.e. the ecological revival of dead spaces. At the same time, they demonstrate that humans can and must act as ‘trustees’ and ‘stewards’ of nature. Where destruction once reigned, responsible action brings new life: water returns, forests grow and people can live with dignity once more.

Giono thus presents a model that anticipates contemporary Western legal debates about the necessity to shift from a anthropocentric to a biocentric legal vision. Rather than withdrawing from nature to protect it, humans must see themselves as an integral part of a whole and take action to restore this integrity.

The text’s significance lies in showing that cultural change is possible. Elzéard demonstrates that individuals influenced by Western culture can develop and embody a biocentric worldview. However, almost twenty years after the publication of this story, Giono seemed to abandon his optimism in a 1970 letter, in view of continuing destruction and human inertia. The question posed by his work therefore remains relevant: can we regain confidence in the power of the individual to act—not as an illusion, but as a concrete obligation to act as a trustee?

In the continuity of Juster’s reflections about literature anticipating nature law concepts, Justine Scarlaken investigates in her contribution “From Beaver Alliances to River Parliaments: New Legal Narratives and Interspecies Representation in Contemporary French Literature (2019–2025)” the literary discussions about the possibility to recognize Nature as a legal subject, thus provided with the capacity ot receive rights. In the face of the Anthropocene crisis, contemporary French literature has emerged as a laboratory for radical legal innovation, transforming rivers and their non-human inhabitants from objects of exploitation into political subjects endowed with rights and democratic representation. This transformation parallels recent legal developments worldwide: in 2017, New Zealand granted the Whanganui River the same legal rights as a person, while Ecuador’s constitution recognizes the rights of nature itself (Tanasescu 2017). Scarlakens chapter examines how recent French works create revolutionary interspecies alliances that both respond to and anticipate such legal paradigm shifts, challenging anthropocentric frameworks and proposing concrete alternatives to environmental destruction. Central to this analysis are two groundbreaking collaborative works: Baptiste Morizot and Suzanne Husky’s *Rendre l’eau à la terre* (2024), which positions the beaver as a “diplomatic ambassador” for river ecosystems, and Camille de Toledo’s *Le fleuve qui voulait écrire: les auditions du Parlement de Loire* (2021), which documents the experimental “Parliament of the Loire” project (2019–2021). These texts exemplify literature’s capacity to function as what Toledo terms a “public service of the imagination”, generating new legal concepts that anticipate and legitimize evolving environmental law.

This analysis reveals how these works operate on multiple interconnected levels to reimagine legal relationships with the natural world. Morizot and Husky fundamentally transform the beaver from pest to partner, presenting it as the “first designer of mega-basins" whose 8-million-year engineering practice offers a model for action liberated from the cult of petroleum, mechanization, and control. Their rehabilitation of non-human knowledge systems as sources of legal and political wisdom provides the conceptual foundation for more radical institutional experiments.

Building on this reconceptualization of interspecies relationships, the "Parliament of the Loire" project represents a unique experiment in democratic representation beyond the human, directly inspired by the legal precedent of the Whanganui River's personhood in New Zealand. Through public hearings and collective deliberation, this initiative explored how rivers, forests, and ecosystems might accede to legal personality and participate in political decision-making. Literature here becomes an institutional laboratory, testing new forms of more-than-human democracy that bridge the gap between legal innovation worldwide and French legal imagination.

These narrative experiments do not remain in the realm of fiction but explicitly identify gaps in current environmental law—rivers treated as property rather than legal subjects—and propose specific legal responses through storytelling. By demonstrating literature's capacity to "point to legal gaps and/or possible legal answers", these works fulfil the mission to examine how Anthropocene literature generates juridical innovations, moving beyond mere description of ecological crisis to active participation in legal transformation.

Drawing on Bruno Latour's anthropology of legal "fabrication" and the advocacy work of "Notre affaire à tous" on rights of nature, this study reveals how contemporary French literature operates as a crucial site of legal imagination. These texts do not merely describe ecological crisis but actively participate in the cultural and conceptual work necessary for legal transformation. The urgency of this literary-legal innovation is underscored by Roberto Epple's observation that in Europe, "less than 3% of rivers remain close to their natural state". Against this backdrop of ecological collapse, literature emerges as a vital force for reimagining the legal foundations of human-nature relationships shifting from anthropocentric to biocentric law.

Matthew H. Birkhold's chapter "I Am the Cold / I Am the Melt": Poetic Testimony and the Right to Be Cold in Jessie Kleemann's *Arkhticós Dolorôs* (2019)" examines how Greenlandic poet and performance artist Jessie Kleemann's poetry collection *Arkhticós Dolorôs* (2021) reimagines the failed legal concept of the 'right to be cold'—itself derived from Sheila Watt-Cloutier's 2005 petition to the Inter-American Commission on Human Rights—as a form of poetic testimony that exposes the epistemological limits of law in addressing climate harm. Rather than treating this juridical failure as merely a defeat to be overcome through better legal argumentation, Birkhold suggests that Kleemann's poetry opens a fundamentally different approach to thinking about responsibility, voice, and justice in an era of planetary crisis.

In 2005, Sheila Watt-Cloutier submitted a groundbreaking petition to the Inter-American Commission on Human Rights on behalf of the Inuit, arguing that climate change constituted a human rights violation because Arctic ice loss threatened Indigenous lifeways, culture, property rights, and subsistence practices. This argument became encapsulated in the phrase 'the right to be cold', which came to signify far more than a juridical innovation in climate governance. It named a fundamental challenge to how law conceptualizes harm, responsibility, and voice in a warming world. However, the petition ultimately failed at the juridical level, unable to surmount the entrenched doctrines of evidence, causation, and jurisdiction that structure legal reasoning. Law demands proof, attribution, and clear territorial boundaries—forms of knowledge that falter when confronted with slow violence, planetary interdependence, and injuries that exceed human scale. As Birkhold notes, "The Arctic could be spoken about, but it could not yet be heard by the law."

Rather than asking how the 'right to be cold' might be successfully formalized within existing legal frameworks, Birkhold turns instead to how Kleemann's poetry reconfigures the failed legal claim as a form of testimony that reconceives the very terms of legal imagination. Originally performed at Blue Lake in 2019 as part of the *At the Moraine* project, the work emerged from Kleemann's sustained engagement with glacier melt and what the project describes as the "distinct language of the ice, the dying glacier." Kleemann's poetry exposes the epistemic assumptions underlying legal knowing and reveals the representational thresholds at which law fails. By exploring what kinds of imagination become possible once we attend to the limits of law's epistemology itself, Birkhold argues that Kleemann's work offers a reorientation of how we might think about justice in the Anthropocene.

The core claim of the chapter is that *Arkhticós Dolorôs* reimagines testimony at three decisive levels, each of which transforms our understanding of what the 'right to be cold' might mean beyond its failed juridical instantiation. First, the collection shifts the 'right to be cold' from a derivative human interest to a more-than-human demand. The Arctic itself—cold itself as a claimant—becomes a rights-bearing subject whose injuries cannot be reduced to human loss. This move recasts the fundamental question: rather than asking how humans can demand a right to cold, the poems ask what it means to listen to the Arctic's own suffering and to recognize it as an entity capable of claiming voice.

Second, the collection reframes responsibility through what Birkhold calls 'global enmeshment', a concept that dissolves the territorial and causal boundaries on which jurisdiction conventionally depends. Rather than relying on the legal fictions of clear attribution and bounded jurisdiction, Kleemann's work redistributes responsibility across linguistic, ecological, and geopolitical networks. This reframes the question of who bears responsibility for Arctic harm not as a matter of legal causation or territorial jurisdiction but as a question of planetary interdependence.

Third, the collection asks whether a different form of legality might emerge from practices that do not presume full comprehension—what Birkhold calls 'a law adequate to the unknown'. Kleemann's multilingual poetics, written in Greenlandic, Danish, and English, deliberately stages an encounter with the conditions of partial understanding. This approach stages an encounter with the conditions under which legal knowledge itself is produced and reveals how legal epistemology is limited by its demand for certainty and full intelligibility.

Methodologically, Birkhold approaches *Arkhticós Dolorôs* not as an intentional legal intervention but as a critical reorganization of law's imaginative terrain. Unlike poetry that deliberately inserts itself into the legal order through explicit arguments about rights and justice, Kleemann's work is not explicitly juridical. Instead, it recreates the imaginative conditions under which law apprehends harm and voice, staging an encounter with opacity and the limits of understanding. By doing so, the poetry models what a jurisprudence might look like if it could work with uncertainty and incompleteness rather than suppressing them as obstacles to be overcome.

In conclusion of this special edition, Amitabh Vikram Dwivedi combines in "Ecocide as Speech Act: How Anthropocene Narratives Perform New Crimes into Legal Thinkability" the speech-act theory (how utterances produce social reality) with law-and-literature approaches to narrative jurisprudence, and with Anthropocene thought that destabilizes the subject/object split and repositions agency across humans, infrastructures, and earth systems. Speech-act and performativity frameworks help explain why 'naming' ecocide matters: it is not descriptive but world-making, generating categories of harm and claimable injury. Narrative jurisprudence clarifies how plot, voice, and genre simulate legal reasoning (standing, causation, precedent, proportionality) and teach readers what a just procedure might look like. Anthropocene relational ontology (human–nonhuman entanglement) then grounds the chapter's central move: ecocide narratives often treat ecosystems as injured parties and climate as an actor, pressing law toward new legal subjects, new kinds of evidence, and responsibility that is collective, scalar, and temporally extended.

Methodologically, the chapter tracks 'ecocide speech acts' across four layers: (1) lexical naming (crime-words, thresholds, definitions), (2) victim construction (who/what can be harmed, who can speak), (3) culpability scripting (chains of causation, intent vs. recklessness, corporate impunity), and (4) procedural imagination (courts, commissions, tribunals, documentation regimes). Key secondary conversations include ecocide advocacy and environmental criminal law, green criminology, environmental humanities, and law-and-literature scholarship on narrative's role in legal consciousness.

The core analysis is anchored in two published book-length narratives that are especially rich in proto-legal imagination. First, Kim Stanley Robinson's *The Ministry for the Future* (2020) is read as a climate-governance novel that repeatedly stages the legal problem of mass harm at planetary scale: it experiments with institutional voice (a quasi-UN ministry), policy instruments, and implicit debates around whether catastrophic ecological damage should be prosecuted as a crime, all while dramatizing the evidentiary and jurisdictional dilemmas of attributing responsibility across states, corporations, and infrastructures. Second, Indra Sinha's *Animal's People* (2007) is read as a victim-cantered legal counter-archive that exposes how corporate disaster and toxic afterlives evade legal remedy; its narration performs a forensic ethics of injury, making the long duration of contamination and the fragmentation of culpability narratable as a single continuing wrong that resembles ecocide in structure even when law refuses the term. Around these, the chapter briefly situates additional relevant texts as comparative satellites: Richard Powers's *The Overstory* (2018) for the trial/activism interface and forest personhood imaginaries; Margaret Atwood's *MaddAddam* books for corporate biocrime and species loss; and Andri Snær Magnason's *On Time and Water* (English trans. 2020/2021) as a nonfictional example where ‘ecocide’ is explicitly proposed as a term that should enter public and legal vocabulary.

All five contributions reveal the presence of ‘legal drafts’ behind literary texts that explore various concepts of responsibility for harm to nature, the recognition of rights for non-humans, the human duty to care for non-humans, and the potential to prosecute harm to nature as ‘ecocide’. As the field of ‘legal drafts’ in Anthropocene literature has barely been investigated to date, the aim and hope of this special edition is to encourage further research in this highly relevant area.

References

Andersen, Gregers. 2020. *Climate Fiction and Cultural Analysis: A New Perspective of Life in the Anthropocene*. New York: Routledge.

Arte. 2021. “Entretiens avec Bruno Latour 2”, 2021. https://www.arte.tv/fr/videos/106738-002-A/entretiens-avec-bruno-latour-2/ (accessed on 7 December 2025, the emission has been cancelled).

Baciagalupi, Paolo. 2016. *Water Knife*. New York: Orbit.

Bareis, Alexander. 2014. Die Make-Believe-Theorie nach Walton. In *Fiktionalität. Ein interdisziplinäres Handbuch*, ed. Tobias Klauk und Tilmann Köppe, 50–67. Berlin, Boston: De Gruyter.

Barrau, Aurélien. 2023. *L'Hypothèse K*. Paris: Grasset.

Baßler, Moritz. 2013. Realismus–Serialität–Fantastik. In *Poetiken der Gegenwart. Deutschsprachige Romane nach 2000*, ed. Silke Horstkotte and Leonhard Herrmann, 31–46. Berlin: De Gruyter.

Böschen, Stefan, and Willy Viehöver. 2012. Narrative Autorität und Wissensproduktion. In *Erzählung und Geltung. Wissenschaft zwischen Autorschaft und Autorität*, ed. Safia Azzouni et al., 303–336. Weilerswist: Velbrück Wissenschaft.

Böttcher, Sven. 2011. *Prophezeiung*. Köln: Kiepenheuer & Witsch.

Chakrabarty, Dipesh. 2018. Anthropocene Time. *History and Theory 57* (1): 5–32.

Cochet, Yves. 2019. *Devant l'effondrement: essai de collapsologie*. Paris: Actes Sud.

Colebrook, Claire. 2014. *Death of the PostHuman: Essays on Extinction*. Vol. 1. Michigan: Open Humanities Press.

Crutzen, Paul J. 2006. „Albedo enhancement by stratospheric sulfur injections: a contribution to resolve a policy dilemma? “. *Climatic change* 77/3-4, pp. 211–220.

Crutzen, Paul J. 2002. Geology of Mankind. *Nature* 415 (6867): 23–24.

Crutzen, Paul J. 2019. In *Das Anthropozän. Schlüsseltexte des Nobelpreisträgers für das neue Erdzeitalter*, ed. Michael Müller. München: oekom.

Crutzen, Paul J., and Will Steffen. 2003. How Long Have We Been in the Anthropocene Era? *Climatic Change* 61:251–257.

Crutzen, Paul J., and Eugene F. Stoermer. 2000. The ‘Anthropocene’. *IGBP- Newsletter* 41:17–18.

Crutzen, Paul J. / Will Steffen. 2021. „How Long Have We Been in the Anthropocene Era?”, in: Paul J. Crutzen and the Anthropocene: A New Epoch in Earth's History. The Anthropocene: Politik — Economics — Society — Science, vol. 1. Cham: Springer, pp. 39–45.

de Toledo, Camille. 2021. *Le Fleuve qui voulait écrire: Les auditions du parlement de Loire*. Paris: Manuella Éditions.

Dürbeck, Gabriele. 2018a. Das Anthropozän erzählen: Fünf Narrative. *Aus Politik und Zeitgeschichte: Klima* 21–23:11–17.

Dürbeck, Gabriele. 2018b. Narrative des Anthropozän – Systematisierung eines interdisziplinären Diskurses. *Kulturwissenschaftliche Zeitschrift* 3 (1): 1–20.

Eco, Umberto. 1994. *Im Wald der Fiktionen. Sechs Streifzüge durch die Literatur*. München, Wien: Hanser Verlag.
Edric, Robert. 2010. *Salvage*. New York: Doubleday.
Edwards, Paul N. 2015. Wissensinfrastrukturen für das Anthropozän. In *Das Anthropozän. Zum Stand der Dinge*, ed. Jürgen Renn and Bernd Scherer. Berlin: Matthes & Seitz.
Esselborn, Hans. 2019. *Die Erfindung der Zukunft in der Literatur: vom technisch-utopischen Zukunftsroman zur deutschen Science-Fiction*. Würzburg: Königshausen & Neumann.
Ghosh, Amitav. 2017. *Die große Verblendung: Der Klimawandel als das Undenkbare*. München: Karl Blessing.
Glass, Rodge. 2013. "Global Warming": The Rise of Cli-fi. In *The Guardian*, 31. Mai 2013.
Goodbody, Axel, and Adeline Johns-Putra. *2018. CliFi. A Companion*. London: Peter Lang.
Goodbody, Axel, and Adeline Johns-Putra. 2019. The Rise of the Climate Change Novel. In *Climate and Literature*, ed. Adeline Johns-Putra, 229–245. Cambridge: Cambridge University Press.
Häberle, Peter. 1983. *Das Grundgesetz der Literaten. Der Verfassungsstaat im (Zerr?) Spiegel der Schönen Literatur*. Baden-Baden: Nomos.
Hamilton, Clive. 2016. The Theodicy of the "Good Anthropocene". *Environmental Humanities 7* (1): 233–238.
Heise, Ursula K. 2008. *Sense of Place and Sense of Planet: The Environmental Imagination of the Global*. New York/Oxford: University Press.
Hüpkes, Philip. 2020. Tiefenzeit. In *Grundbegriffe des Anthropozän. Ein interdisziplinäres Lexikon des DFG-Forschungsprojekts 2020*, ed. Gabriele Dürbeck, 1–8. Open-Access Lexikon. https://doi.org/10.23660/voado-233 (accessed on 7 December 2025).
Ironmonger, John. 2019. *Der Wal und das Ende der Welt*. Frankfurt am Main: Fischer.
Ironmonger, John. 2021. *Das Jahr des Dugongs*. Frankfurt am Main: Fischer.
Ironmonger, John. 2023. *Der Eisbär und die Hoffnung von morgen*. Frankfurt am Main: Fischer.
Itäranta, Emmy. 2014. *Memory of Water*. New York: Harper Collins.
IUGS. 2024. "The Anthropocene", 20.03.2024. https://www.iugs.org/_files/ugd/f1fc07_40d1a7ed58de458c9f8f24de5e739663.pdf?index=true (accessed on 12 December 2025).
Jacquenod-Desforges, Claudine. 2022. Comment parler des villes du futur? Science-fiction, prospective et collapsologie. In *Science-fiction et mondes urbains*, ed. Jérôme Goffette, 145–164. Norderstedt: Books on Demand.
Kalies, Grit. 2019. *Raumzeit*. Halle: mitteldeutscher Verlag.
Kiefer, Gabriele. 2019. *Platz der Engel*. Leipzig: Zweitausendeins.
Kindt, Tom. 2011. 'Das Unmögliche, das dennoch geschieht': Zum Begriff der literarischen Phantastik am Beispiel von Werken Thomas Manns. *Thomas Mann Jahrbuch 24*:44–56.
Kingsolver, Barbara. 2013. *Flights Behavior*. London: Faber & Faber.
Klauk, Tobias, and Tilmann Köppe. 2014. *Fiktionalität: Ein interdisziplinäres Handbuch*. Vol. 4. Berlin: De Gruyter.
Klein, Christian. 2013. Erzählung. In *Literatur und Wissen. Ein interdisziplinäres Handbuch*, ed. Roland Bogards et al., 17–21. Stuttgart/Weimar: Metzler.
Klein, Christian, and Matías Martínez. 2009. *Wirklichkeitserzählungen. Felder, Formen und Funktionen nicht-literarischen Erzählens*. Stuttgart: Metzler.
Klein, Thomas. 2020. Enkeltauglich. Realistische Utopien im Zeichen des Klimawandels. *DIEGESIS. Interdisziplinäres E-Journal für Erzählforschung / Interdisciplinary E-Journal for Narrative Research* 9 (2): 39–51.
Koenig, Gaspar. 2023. *Humus*. Paris: J'ai lu.
Latour, Bruno. 2015. *Face à Gaia: Huit conférences sur le nouveau régime climatique*. Paris: La Découverte.
Liljestrand, Jens. 2022. *Der Anfang von morgen*. Frankfurt am Main: Fischer.
Lloyd, Saci. 2009. *Carbon Diaries 2015*. New York: Holiday House.
Lovelock, James. 2016. Gaia: A new look at life on earth. Oxford: Oxford University Press, 2016.

Lunde, Maja. 2018. The History of Bees. London: Scribner.
Lunde, Maja. 2019. The End of the Ocean. London: Scribner.
Lunde, Maja. 2022. The Last Wild Horses. New York: Simon & Schuster.
Lunde, Maja. 2025. The Dream of a Tree. London: Scribner.
Lynch, Jonathan P. 2007. Roots of the second green revolution. *Australian Journal of Botany 55* (5): 493–512.
MacDonald, Gordon, et al. 1979. The Long Term Impact of Atmospheric Carbon Dioxide on Climate. In *Technical Report JSR-78-07*, Washington, U.S. Department of Energy, 1979.
Magnason, Andri Snaer. 2021. On Time and Water. A History of Our Future. London: Serpent's Tail.
Malkmus, Bernhard. 2015. Naturgeschichten vom Fisch, oder: Die Angst vor dem Anthropozän. *Scheidewege* 45:183–200.
Mayer, Sylvie. 2015. Klimawandelroman. In *Ecocriticism: Eine Einführung*, ed. Gabriele Dürbeck and Urte Stobbe, 233–244. Köln/Weimar/Wien: Böhlau Verlag.
McEwan, Ian. 2011. *Solar*. London: Vintage.
Müller-Dietz, Heinz. 1990. *Grenzüberschreitungen. Beiträge zur Beziehung zwischen Literatur und Recht*. Baden-Baden: Nomos.
Nesselhauf, Jonas. 2020. Grundbegriffe des Anthropozän. Ein interdisziplinäres Lexikon des DFG-Forschungsprojekts 'Narrative des Anthropozän in Wissenschaft und Literatur'. In *Open Access Lexikon,* ed. Gabriele Dürbeck, 1–6.
Oreskes, Naomi, and Erik M. Conway. 2013. The Collapse of Western Civilization: A View from the Future. *Daedalus 142* (1): 40–58.
Ostheimer, Jochen. 2020. Den eigenen Untergang erzählen, um ihn zu verhindern. *LIMINA - Grazer theologische Perspektiven* 3 (1): 41–61.
Römer, Inga. 2012. 'Wirklichkeitserzählungen' als Forschungsfeld der Narratologie. Rezension zu Klein, Christian, and Matías Martínez. Wirklichkeitserzählungen. Felder, Formen und Funktionen nicht-literarischen Erzählens JB Metzler, Stuttgart, 2009. *DIEGESIS. Interdisziplinäres E-Journal für Erzählforschung / Interdisciplinary E-Journal for Narrative Research* 1 (1): 104–108.
Searle, John R. 1975. The logical status of fictional discourse. *New Literary History 6* (2): 319–332.
Schwägerl, Christian. 2012. Menschenzeit. Zerstören oder gestalten? Wie wir heute die Welt von morgen erschaffen. München: Goldmann, 2012.
Sloterdijk, Peter. 2015. Das Anthropozän–Ein Prozeß-Zustand am Rande der Erd-Geschichte. *Das Anthropozän. Zum Stand der Dinge* 2:25–44.
Stanley Robinson, Kim. 2018. *New York*. London: Orbit.
Stanley Robinson, Kim. 2020. *The Ministry for the Future*. Orbit.
Steffen, Will, et al. 2007. The Anthropocene: Are Humans Now Overwhelming the Great Forces of Nature? *Ambio* 36 (8): 614–621.
Steffen, Will, et al. 2015. The Trajectory of the Anthropocene: The Great Acceleration. *The Anthropocene Review* 2 (1): 81–98.
Stengers, Isabelle. 2016. Accepting the Reality of Gaia: A Fundamental Shift? In *The Anthropocene and the Global Environmental Crisis*, 134–144. New York: Routledge.
Stoppani, Antonio. 1873. *Corso di Geologia del professore Antonio Stoppani*. Vol. III. Milan: Bernardoni/Brigola.
Todorov, Tzvetan. 1970. *Introduction à la littérature fantastique*. Paris: Seuil.
Trojanow, Ilija. 2011. *Eistau*. München: Hanser.
Tschischwitz, Heiko. 2022. *Die Welt kippt*. Berlin: List Paul.
Vernadsky, Vladimir I. 1998. *The Biosphere, translated and annotated version from the original of 1926*. New York: Springer.
Viehöver, Willy. 2011. Governing the Planetary Greenhouse in Spite of Scientific Uncertainty. *Science, Technology & Innovation Studies* 6 (2): 127–154.
Viehöver, Willy. 2012. Öffentliche Erzählungen und der globale Wandel des Klimas. In *Erzählungen im Öffentlichen. Über die Wirkung von narrativen Diskursen*, ed. Markus Arnold et al., 173–215. Wiesbaden: Springer.

Welzer, Harald, and Klaus Wiegandt, eds. 2011. *Perspektiven einer nachhaltigen Entwicklung. Wie sieht die Welt im Jahr 2050 aus?* Frankfurt am Main: Fischer.
Zalasiewicz, Jan, et al. 2024. The Anthropocene within the Geological Time Scale: A Response to Fundamental Questions. *IUGS Episodes – Journal of International Geoscience* 47 (1): 65–83.
Zipfel, Frank. 2014. Fiktionssignale. In *Fiktionalität. Ein interdisziplinäres Handbuch*, ed. Tobias Klauk and Tilmann Köppe, 97–124. Berlin, Boston: *De Gruyter*.

The Principle of Responsibility in Climate Novels: An Encounter Between Literature and Law

Alexandra Juster

Abstract Literature provides a means of precisely observing social contexts, needs, crises, fears, desires and hopes. While the law regulates situations and circumstances at a specific point in history, literature highlights legal inconsistencies, shortcomings and gaps, and anticipates legal needs. Drawing on the relationship between law and literature, this chapter aims to 'extract' the legally relevant discourse on individual and collective responsibility in the Anthropocene from three literary texts: *Platz der Engel* (2019) by Gabriele Kiefer; *Humus* (2024) by Gaspard Koenig; and *Der Eisbär und die Hoffnung auf Morgen* (2023)—*The Wager and the Bear (2021)*—by John Ironmonger. This approach aims to make literary references and approaches to the Anthropocene fruitful for legal and ethical considerations. First, the concept of responsibility in the legal sense will be presented. Then, reference will be made to previous legal and ethical considerations of responsibility in connection with climate change. Finally, a more detailed analysis of the discourse on responsibility in the three climate novels will be provided.

Keywords Anthropocene · Responsibility · Law · Ethics · Climate literature

This chapter focuses on the legal and ethical discourse surrounding responsibility for climate damage as depicted in literature. The complexity and difficulty of determining the subject and object of these environmental responsibilities will be illustrated through an analysis of three novels: *Platz der Engel* (2019) by Gabriele *Kiefer, Humus* (2024) by Gaspard Koenig, and *Der Eisbär und die Hoffnung auf morgen*—in English *The Wager and the Bear* (2021)—by John Ironmonger. Our study of these literary discourses will involve a detailed analysis of the texts,[1] paying particular attention to patterns in the description of events related to

[1] Cf. Keller (2018), p. 200.

A. Juster (✉)
University of Innsbruck, Innsbruck, Austria
e-mail: Alexandra.Juster@uibk.ac.at

A. Juster (ed.), *Legal Drafts in Anthropocene Literature*, SpringerBriefs in Law,
https://doi.org/10.1007/978-3-032-27283-6_2

environmental responsibility.[2] Our aim is to highlight not only the obvious discourse on climate responsibility, but also the subtle details that are barely noticeable in isolation, but which become apparent when considered in their context.[3]

This contribution aims therefore to explore the concept of individual and collective responsibility for the consequences of human-caused climate change and to derive indications and suggestions for potential future legal regulations or sanctions for irresponsible behaviour.

However, before attempting to derive this legally significant discourse from the literary texts, it seems necessary to first examine the current legal concept of responsibility for human-caused damage in the Anthropocene era. This background information will then inform the analysis of each text.

1 On the Principle of Responsibility

According to Ludger Heidbrink, responsibility is the voluntary or rule-compliant assumption of responsibility by a competent or accountable actor for the consequences of their actions in relation to an applicable norm.[4] Responsibility arises from the causal connection between the action of an accountable perpetrator and the damage caused, in conjunction with the normative or moral obligation to (re)compensate for it. At the legal level, the concept of responsibility derives from the obligation not to violate provisions of a normative nature. At the ethical and moral level responsibility arises from the obligation towards society. Jean-Paul Sartre already postulated that "each of us [...] is guilty towards everyone, for everyone and for everything".[5] A prerequisite for the attribution of responsibility is the accountability of the person acting, which results from the sequence of freedom—causality—intentionality—knowledge of the possible consequences of action, which Aristotle already recognised:[6] In order to assert a claim to responsibility, an action must be free, i.e. without coercion, and conscious, whereby the result of this action must be directly attributable to the acting subject (principle of causality). However, the criteria and standards for the concrete attribution of responsibility depend on the framework conditions under which an action takes place (intent, purpose, abilities, tasks, roles, regulations, etc.), i.e. they depend on whether the action follows legal, moral or task-related imperatives.[7] If a responsible person is considered accountable, they are liable because of the *consequence-based principle of legitimacy* for past, present and/or foreseeable future consequences of their actions.[8]

---

[2] Cf. Konersmann (2021), p. 84.

[3] Cf. Juster (2025), pp. 48–62.

[4] Cf. Heidbrink (2017), p. 11.

[5] Sartre (1988), p. 165.

[6] Cf. Heidbrink (2017), p. 9.

[7] Cf. ibid., p. 10.

[8] Cf. ibid., p. 13.

Responsibility in the Anthropocene era,[9] as a phase of dramatic resource depletion, water, air and soil contamination, destruction of biodiversity, water and food shortages, and climate deregulation of the oceans and continents with devastating consequences for humans and animals, means an individual and collective obligation to save what can be saved and to do everything possible to halt the worsening of life-threatening conditions. In this context, Eva Horn and Hannes Bergthaller rightly point to the problem of the global dimension of the phenomenon, which can only be influenced by the "cumulative effective power of human action" and not by individual, isolated action.[10]

The German *Advisory Council on Global Change* (WBGU) provides a summary of the significant challenges that humanity is facing in the Anthropocene, which requires

> a 'Great Transformation'. The central requirements of this comprehensive transformation arise from the limits of the Earth system, which force a restructuring of national economies and the global economy within these limits to avoid irreversible damage to global ecosystems and its effects on humanity. Production, consumption patterns and lifestyles must be changed in such a way that greenhouse gas emissions are reduced to a minimum over the coming decades (decarbonisation of energy systems and the creation of climate-friendly societies), essential resource scarcities (especially land, water, strategic mineral resources) can be minimised through significant increases in resource efficiency, and abrupt changes in the Earth system (tipping points) can be avoided through economic and development strategies that take into account the planetary boundaries.[11]

From this challenging situation arises everyone's ethical obligation to prevent or at least to milder the Anthropocene effects, which Paul Crutzen and Eugene Stormer declared to be a man-made catastrophe.[12] Will Steffen & al. call for responsible action,[13] Peter Sloterdijk and Dipesh Chakrabarty question the blame and cause of this situation,[14] Gabriele Dürbeck formulates a general principle of responsibility in the Anthropocene:

> The term 'Anthropocene' refers to a new geological epoch in which humanity has the dominant geophysical influence on the Earth system, and from this, human responsibility for the future of the planet is derived. The concept also contains a call to redefine humanity's position in relation to nature and the cosmos and to use limited natural resources responsibly.[15]

In view of the urgent need to decarbonise energy supplies, reduce emissions of CO2, methane and other gases, and ban pollutants in agriculture as the main cause of global warming and species extinction, Uwe Schneidewind calls for a "great

[9] See on the history of the concept of Anthropocene: Wallenhorst (2024), pp. 73–91.

[10] Horn and Bergthaller (2019), p. 18.

[11] Wissenschaftlicher Beirat der Bundesregierung (2011), p. 3.

[12] Cf. Crutzen and Stormer (2000), pp. 17–18.

[13] Cf. Steffen et al. (2015), p. 94.

[14] Cf. Sloterdijk (2015), pp. 25–44.

[15] Dürbeck (2018), p. 11.

transformation",[16] reducing economic growth and the quantity of material consumption.[17]

In his narrative *Wasser und Zeit: Eine Geschichte unserer Zukunft* (2020), Andri Snaer Magnason refers to the responsibility of the richest ten per cent of the world's population, who are responsible for half of all CO2 emissions.[18] According to Magnason, it is therefore essential to determine the responsibility and costs for remedying environmental and climate damage.[19] But this is precisely where the difficulty lies: how exactly should the perpetrators be identified? How exactly can the damage caused be measured? How should the amount of damage be determined? Who, which institution, which court is responsible for this? Magnason proposes introducing legal recourse with the term 'ecocide' as a criminal offence: "Ecocide is a new term, analogous to genocide. With ecocide laws, it would be possible to hold those involved in the destruction of ecosystems accountable".[20] Gerhard Kruip proposes politically enforceable regulatory mechanisms and controls at the collective level, joint binding regulations through self-commitment in the form of institutions, incentive mechanisms such as tax measures and subsidies, penalties and international cooperation. Companies, trade unions, churches, religious communities and the media can make responsible decisions and act accordingly. At the individual level, according to Kruip, it is the responsibility of each citizen to reduce their "ecological footprint"[21] through individual decisions.[22] The most effective approach would be a shared sense of ethical responsibility, setting aside selfish interests and a willingness to cooperate for success, according to the motto "with united forces", as clearly illustrated by the "prisoner's dilemma".[23] In *L'Hypothèse K.* (2023), Aurélien Barrau calls on science to conduct science in a more responsible manner, free from primarily capitalist considerations.[24] This brief overview of considerations regarding the principle of responsibility in the Anthropocene demonstrates the complexity and extreme difficulty of capturing it and putting it into

[16] Schneidewind (2018).

[17] Cf. Kruip (2020), pp. 30–31; cf. also Skidelsky and Skidelsky (2012).

[18] Cf. Magnason (2020), p. 186.

The English translation has been published 2021 under the title *On Time and Water*.

[19] Ibid.

[20] Ibid., p. 230.

[21] Kruip (2020), pp. 32–34; cf. also Wackernagel and Beyers (2016).

[22] Cf. Kruip (2020), pp. 34–37.

[23] Aßländer (2022), p. 715.

The prisoner's dilemma demonstrates that cooperation is the most profitable strategy for everyone involved. The basic model is relatively simple. Two prisoners are charged with a crime they committed together. As they are imprisoned separately, they have no opportunity to agree on a joint defence strategy. If they cooperate and remain silent, they can be sentenced to two years' imprisonment for a minor offence. However, if one defendant incriminates the other while the other remains silent and cooperative, the leniency rule applies: the lenient witness goes unpunished while the other defendant is sentenced to fifteen years' imprisonment. If both defendants are uncooperative and incriminate each other, they will both be sentenced to ten years' imprisonment.

[24] Cf. Barrau (2023), p. 33.

practice. The following chapter will briefly outline how international and national legal systems are addressing this challenge, using random samples. Random because the volume of legal contributions, draft legislation, normative texts, legal commentaries and analyses, as well as the scope of legal actions and case law, has increased exponentially in recent years and can therefore only be presented in a very inadequate and sketchy manner within this contribution.

2 Sketches on Law in the Anthropocene

At the international level, the Paris Climate Agreement of 12 December 2015 commits 197 countries to take measures to limit global warming to 1.5 °C, or a maximum of 2 °C.[25] A rulebook adopted at COP24 in Katowice in 2018 contains binding regulations on the level of climate protection contributions, transparency in reporting on climate protection measures and global stocktaking. The Paris Climate Agreement provides a first serious reference framework for determining the responsibilities and rule violations of states, companies and collectives in the Anthropocene by setting climate targets such as limiting global warming to a maximum of 1.5–2 °C.

At German level, article 20a of the Constitution (Grundgesetz GG) requires the state to protect the natural foundations of life. It states that "the state shall also protect the natural foundations of life and animals within the framework of the constitutional order through legislation, and in accordance with the law and justice through the executive power and the judiciary, in responsibility for future generations". On 24 March 2021, the German Federal Constitutional Court (BVerfG) passed a resolution based on Article 20a GG, recognising the obligation of current generations to avoid shifting the greenhouse gas burden to future generations,[26] for their benefit, with overall responsibility lying with the federal states (Bundesländer) and not with the federal government (Bund).[27] (38) The guidelines and emission values to be observed are those of the *Paris Climate Agreement*. The Supreme Court also emphasises that the state 'cannot escape from its responsibility by pointing to greenhouse gas emissions in other countries."[28]

In a ruling dated 9 October 2018, a district court in The Hague (Netherlands) already emphasised the state's obligation to offer its citizens "protection against the

---

[25] See the Paris Agreement of 12 December 2025: https://unfccc.int/sites/default/files/english_paris_agreement.pdf (accessed on 12 November 2025).

[26] Cf. Frenz (2023), p. 159 and pp. 162–217.

See the decision by the German Constitutional Court: BVerfG, Beschl. v. 24. 03. 2021 – 1 BvR 2656/18 u. a.

[27] See the decision by the German Constitutional Court: BVerfG, Beschl. v. 18. 01. 2022 – 1 BvR 1565/21, 1 BvR 1566/21 u. a., NJW 2022, 844, Rn. 12 ff.

[28] See the decision by the German Constitutional Court: BVerfG, Beschl. v. 24. 03. 2021 – 1 BvR 2656/18 u. a., p. 1. See also: Sinder (2021), pp. 1078–1086.

concrete threat posed by climate change in the form of risks such as flooding, disease, drought, forest fires, drinking water shortages and damage to the ecosystem […]; it must do everything in its power, even if it cannot save the global climate on its own".[29] On 26 May 2021, the same Dutch court ordered Shell to reduce its CO2 emissions by 45% by 2030.[30]

In France, environmental and climate protection was elevated to constitutional status in 2005 in the form of a 10-article environmental charter.[31] Since 2006, this constitutional environmental charter has been considered in French case law.[32]

In fact, there has been an increase in 'climate lawsuits' in recent years, with citizens or NGOs attempting to force governments or powerful corporations to withdraw environmentally harmful measures, repair environmental damage or prevent it. There is a growing demand for an individual right to preserve an environment that enables healthy and dignified living and working conditions—in short, an environment that makes life possible.[33] A now well-known example of such an individual legal claim in Germany is the lawsuit brought by Peruvian farmer Saúl Luciano Lliuya against the German energy company RWE, on the grounds that the CO2 emissions caused by RWE in Peru are melting the Palcacocha glacier in the Andes and that the meltwater is threatening his house, his village of Huaraz and his livelihood. On 28 May 2025, the Higher Regional Court of Hamm rejected Saúl's claim for compensation on the grounds that the future flood damage was not specific enough, but at the same time opened the possibility of holding environmentally damaging corporations accountable across borders.[34]

A second significant breakthrough in recognising the protection of natural resources as a fundamental right was achieved by a decision of the European Court of Human Rights (ECHR). Although the ECHR has not yet gone so far as to grant individuals the right to bring legal action, it has taken the groundbreaking step of granting civil collectives and associations the right to bring class actions. The specific case concerned a Swiss association of senior citizens who had unsuccessfully argued before the Swiss courts that Switzerland was taking insufficient measures to

---

[29] See the decisions by the Dutch Court in The Hague: District Court of The Hague, Uitspraak op 9 October 2018 – 200.178.245/01, ECLI:NL: GHDHA:2018:2591; similarly: District Court of The Hague, Judgment of 20 December 2019 – 19/00135, ECLI:NL:HR: 2019:2007, para. 5.7.7.

[30] See the decision by the Dutch Court in The Hague: District Court of The Hague, Judgment of 26 May 2021 – C/09/571932/HA ZA 19-379, ECLI:NL:RBDHA:2021:5337.

[31] French Constitutional Law No. 2005-205 of 1 March 2005.

[32] On the French 'Charte de l'environnement', see: https://www.legifrance.gouv.fr/contenu/menu/droit-national-en-vigueur/constitution/charte-de-l-environnement (accessed 12 November 2025).

[33] See the Climate Change Litigation Database of the Sabin Centre for Climate Change Law at Columbia Law School https://climatecasechart.com/non-us-climate-change-litigation/ (accessed on 19 October 2025) and the database of the Grantham Research Institute on Climate Change and the Environment at the London School of Economics on global legislation and strategy on climate issues: https://climate-laws.org/ (accessed on 19 October 2025).

[34] See the decision by the German Court of Appeal Hamm: OLG Hamm, 28.05.2025 – 5 U 15/17. https://dejure.org/dienste/vernetzung/rechtsprechung?Text=5%20U%2015/17#Entscheidung2 (accessed on 17 December 2025).

reduce global warming and was thereby seriously endangering the health and living conditions of senior citizens, many of whom are over 80 years old (e.g. through climate-related heat waves).[35] This violated Article 8 of the European Convention on Human Rights (ECHR), which expressly provides for the right of individuals to "effective protection by the state authorities against the (…) effects of climate change on their lives, health, well-being and quality of life".[36]

In conclusion of this section, it can be said that the 2015 *Paris Climate Agreement* has probably had a global accelerating effect on the framework legislation for curbing global warming, and that since then, initiatives for the legal protection of the foundations of human life for present and future generations have multiplied at the constitutional, national and judicial levels. This involves the struggle for the recognition of at least a collective and, better still, an individual right to an environment worth living in. These statements reflect the need to recognise national, collective and individual responsibility for harmful actions. However, it seems that law alone is insufficient to address the global challenges of the Anthropocene. Rather, it requires a strong ethical commitment to motivate people to counter the climate crisis through individual and collective actions where law does not operate.

3 Sketches on Ethics in the Anthropocene

The law is first and foremost a social phenomenon that is intended to regulate social relations in such a way that peaceful coexistence in society is possible. In this context, Jorge Viñuales states that, in its numerous regulatory functions, the law has primarily promoted economic activities and failed to prevent the effects of the Anthropocene.[37]

Following on from this 'failure' of the law to prevent climate catastrophe, Marius Bartmann addresses the problem of ethical individual and collective responsibility in the Anthropocene, stating that "there is consensus that climate change is a genuinely ethical problem and raises questions of intra- and intergenerational justice in particular".[38]

Bartmann's reflections are reminiscent of Hans Jonas's object- rather than subject-centred principle of responsibility, which refers to the matter at hand and not to the act of doing something: "according to which I feel responsible not

---

[35] Cf. Amos (2024).

See the decision by the European Court of Human Rights: *EGMR 09.04.2024 (GK), 53600/20, KlimaSeniorinnen ua/Schweiz.*

[36] Lenk (2021), p. 140; see also Jonas (1979), p. 36, note 57.

[37] Cf. Viñuales (2016), p. 21.

[38] Bartmann (2024), p. 121; cf. also: Birnbacher (2012); Birnbacher (2015); Birnbacher (2022); Roser and Seidel (2015); Hahn and Schnitker (2017); Wallimann-Helmer (2017); Bazargan-Forward and Tollefsen (2020); Bartmann and Halsband (2023); Keij and van Meurs (2023).

primarily for my behaviour and its consequences, but for the thing that my actions affect".[39] With this shift from subject to object, Jonas means the extension of the principle of responsibility from the polluter to a "fiduciary or custodial responsibility of humans" to protect nature and creatures from danger.[40] In this way, collective responsibility adds to individual responsibility.

When it comes to the individual action demanded by Jonas, the question arises as to the direct attribution of damage contributions (e.g. in the form of CO2 emissions) to the actions of individuals according to the principle of causality of responsibility. The question arises as to how the harmfulness of individual actions can be measured and whether these can be considered harmful on a global scale at all. In the specific context of the Anthropocene, Bartmann argues that it makes little sense to insist on the principle of the "causal nexus between individual actions and potential climate change damage".[41] Rather, should "moral responsibility be established on a non-causal basis (e.g. through considerations of fairness)".[42] Elisabeth Cripps proposes a different approach to individual responsibility, according to which individuals should be held responsible if their individual actions, in conjunction with other individual actions, cause harm, even if the individual action alone would not cause such a harm.[43] Regarding the question of how to measure the extent of harmful actions by individuals or groups, Marius Bartmann suggests resolving this dilemma from the perspective of the limited resource of the atmosphere. For this purpose, we could refer to the remaining CO_2 budget of approximately 250 gigatonnes of carbon dioxide equivalents, in accordance with the *Paris Agreement's* provision*s*. This means, according to Bartmann, orienting oneself towards quantifiable tolerance limits, "the exceeding of which would have intolerable consequences today or in the future [...]".[44] With the establishment of a normative framework, it can be assumed that everyone has an obligation to their fellow human beings and future generations to keep their contribution to the consumption of this CO2 budget as low as possible to avoid the depletion of the CO2 capital. Such a moral obligation corresponds to the duty not to expose other people to unnecessary risks to their health or property, as Sven Ove Hansson puts it: "Everyone has a prima facie a moral right not to be exposed to risk of negative impact, such as damage to his health and his property, through the actions of others".[45]

Regarding the experience of German National Socialism, Karl Jaspers sees collective guilt "in the way of life of a population"[46] as culpable participation, which also arises from small and minute actions as well as omissions or passive

---

39 Jonas (1979), p. 174.

40 Cf. Lenk (2021), p. 140.

41 Bartmann (2024), pp. 123–124.

42 Ibid., p. 124.

43 Cf. Cripps (2013), p. 169; see also Parfit (1986).

44 Bartmann (2024), pp. 128–129.

45 Hansson (2007), p. 31.

46 Jaspers (1987), p. 51.

complacency.[47] As Ana Honnacker argues, Jaspers's concept of collective guilt can easily be applied to our Anthropocene era, and in this sense, "ecological guilt", as Honnacker further explains, "has a structural quality and is embedded in a collectively actualised way of life".[48]

The question of responsibility for the consequences of climate change is therefore, as we have attempted to show, extremely complex on an ethical level and difficult to answer unequivocally. A particular challenge is the attribution of climate-damaging actions to their authors.

Against this legal and ethical backdrop, the following section will examine *Platz der Engel*, *Humus* and *Der Eisbär und die Hoffnung auf Morgen*[49] to show how these works convey the ideas of legal and/or ethical question of responsibility in the Anthropocene.

4 Responsibility in Kiefer, Ironmonger and Koenig

The three novels *Platz der Engel* (2019), *Humus* (2024) and *Der Eisbär und die Hoffnung auf morgen* (2023) raise the question of responsibility in the Anthropocene. They touch on law as well as ethics, they concern politics, economic actors and every single citizen. In *Platz der Engel*, the focus shifts to the individual, who finds it difficult to stand up to the eco-giants; in *Humus*, capitalist greed is held primarily responsible, while in *Der Eisbär und die Hoffnung auf morgen*, attention is drawn to political irresponsibility. This will now be discussed in more detail below.

4.1 Platz der Engel

In her novel *Platz der Engel*,[50] Gabriele Kiefer attempts to illustrate the global dimension of the climate catastrophe by making Germany the scene of devastation and life-threatening climate-induced tornadoes. By shifting the climate catastrophe to highly developed Germany, the novel highlights the responsibility of all countries on earth to mitigate the consequences of the Anthropocene. It is no longer possible to turn a blind eye to more distant, 'underdeveloped' and poorer countries while Germany protects itself. Climate-related disaster scenarios affect everyone,

---

[47] Cf. Honnacker (2021), pp. 149–150.

[48] Ibid., p. 153.

[49] My quotes refer to the original German version of *Platz der Engel*, the original French version of Humus, and the German translation *Der Eisbär und die Hoffnung auf morgen* of John Ironmonger's original novel, titled *The Wager and the Bear*. All the translations from French and German into English are mine.

[50] Kiefer (2019).

regardless of whether they are rich or poor; borders are falling, and with them the geographical boundaries of responsibility.

As one of the leading figures in AQUA—a "still young protest movement [...] dedicated to the consequences of climate change and carrying out media-effective actions"[51]—Marie had already dealt intensively with the various technical solutions for reducing global warming caused by CO2 emissions into the atmosphere. She knows that the goals of the *Paris Agreement* were far from being achieved and that climate change was happening even faster than scientists and experts could have imagined.[52] That is why she is campaigning for a radical change in the economy, politics and society, aware that only collective, responsible action towards a new way of life can save the Earth.

Kiefer imagines a measure to promote and simultaneously measure individual responsibility, namely the EU-wide introduction of an energy pass: "The governments of the EU have invoked an emergency law and will require every citizen to have an energy pass that regulates and limits personal CO2 consumption!".[53] The concept of the energy pass is based on the individual recording of CO2 consumption, which is measured and controlled by a points system, whereby a specified upper limit must not be exceeded. If the holder has used up the points quota on their energy pass, they may not use any more points until the energy pass has been regenerated, or they can generate new points by taking special CO2-reducing measures, such as purchasing an electric car, fuel cells or solar-powered devices.[54] Another way to regain points is to volunteer in schools and kindergartens to explain to schoolchildren how the points were lost.[55] The following terms explain further details about the energy pass points system:

> So what counts towards an energy pass? First and foremost, it includes the ecological balance of your purchases. If you buy a banana from South America, the energy consumption for the product is higher than for an apple from your neighbourhood, which does not incur any significant transport costs. However, if the apple from the neighbourhood continues to be stored in an energy-guzzling cold store despite all warnings, the banana may score fewer points if it was transported to us by a hydrogen-powered aeroplane or wind turbine-powered ship.[56]

This echoes Sven Ove Hansson's idea of the responsibility of individuals not to unnecessarily negatively impact the lives of others[57] or, as Bartmann suggests, to at least subject harmful actions to a duty of justification.[58]

---

[51] Ibid., p. 38.

[52] Cf. ibid., p. 21.

[53] Ibid., pp. 29–30.

[54] Cf. ibid., pp. 30–31 and 134.

[55] Cf. ibid., p. 59.

[56] Ibid., p. 31.

[57] Cf. Hansson (2007), p. 31.

[58] Cf. Bartmann (2024), p. 135.

On a legal level, Martha demands in one of her television appearances that every citizen should have a constitutionally enshrined right to an intact climate and, in return, should be liable for violating climate rules: "[…] I demand that every person's right to an intact climate be included in our constitution, including personal liability for gross disregard of climate protection!"[59] Climate offenders should be held accountable, among other things, through community service.[60] Kiefer outlines a fundamental right to the preservation of the foundations of life, as has already been increasingly incorporated into national constitutions and is now also being recognised more frequently by the courts. This raises the issue of personal liability of individuals for environmental damage, but without making any concrete proposals for the detailed design of this individual responsibility, apart from consumption behaviour being rewarded or punished by a points system in the energy pass. Whilst real-world legal and ethical considerations regarding climate responsibility are based on the goals of the *Paris Climate Agreement*, i.e. a specific CO2 budget, to quote Bartmann,[61] Kiefer's energy pass merely sets individual limits for CO2 emissions without considering a global, planetary volume. However, the energy pass proposal could provide ideas for the individual assessment of 'responsibility' if this were placed in a global context with a global cap on CO2 emissions.

Numerous politicians and large corporations do not share this conscious approach to CO2 emissions and, out of their own economic and capitalist interests, do not shy away from preventing Martha's efforts to replace fossil fuels with alternative concepts by publicly exploiting an intimate sex scene between her and Jasper, who is 35 years her junior.[62] The aim is to thwart Martha's possible appointment as EU Commissioner for Climate Issues. Kiefer explicitly denounces here the irresponsible behaviour of powerful corporations that cling to fossil fuels, which contribute so devastatingly to global warming, out of short-term greed for profit. In doing so, she emphasises the imbalance between the 'powerful', who could make a decisive contribution to climate change, and the powerless ordinary citizen.[63]

The irresponsibility of those who have the means to make a decisive contribution to climate change is contrasted with that of individuals, whose responsibility may seem less significant at first glance but, to speak with Elisabeth Cripps, cannot be ignored when considered in conjunction with that of many other individuals.[64] However, the key question remains: how can the powerful eco-giants, who continue to pay little heed to ethical arguments but consume the largest share of the CO2 budget, be forced to change their thinking?

In the following section, we will see that *Humus* by Gaspar Koenig also considers the issue of corporate responsibility for climate damages.

---

[59] Kiefer (2019), p. 282.

[60] Cf. ibid., p. 299.

[61] Cf. Bartmann (2024), pp. 131–135.

[62] Cf. Kiefer (2019), p. 344.

[63] Cf. ibid., p. 280.

[64] Cf. Cripps (2013), p. 69.

4.2 Humus

In *Humus*,[65] Arthur and Kevin, two close friends who graduated from the Paris University of Agricultural Sciences *AgroParisTech*, recall lectures on earthworms by Professor Marcel Combe. He preached that there would be no usable soil without earthworms.[66] Combe's teaching inspires Kevin to think about natural methods of waste disposal and Arthur to take over his grandfather's farm with its soil depleted by artificial fertilisers.[67] Worm cultures are the central solution for both: for Kevin, they ensure the natural conversion of waste into the finest humus; for Arthur, they are intended to transform the barren soil around his grandfather's farm into fertile humus without artificial methods.[68] Kevin tries unsuccessfully[69] to obtain a bank loan to produce a first prototype of a designer worm composter for city dwellers who are seeking to ease their conscience about their daily waste production.[70] According to the banks, to make the worm composter attractive to today's customers, it would have to be at least digitally equipped, a kind of 'smart worm' that can be operated remotely without coming into touch with the worms or the soil. However, as Kevin points out, this would negate the environmental benefits of composting due to the energy consumption involved.[71]

Gaspard Koenig points to this refusal to grant credit for a serious, simple, energy-independent invention that is unattractive by today's standards. He further points to the dominance of ethically questionable economic interests on the one hand and the equally ethically questionable behaviour of modern consumers on the other. Both sides, business and consumers, give themselves a hypocritical veneer of 'greenwashing', but only as long as this does not mean a loss of profit and comfort. The industry is making higher profits from expensive, digitised worm composters, insofar as a digital remote-controlled system guarantees the customer a distance from nature. This means in plain language, that the worms are supposed to offer the advantage of ecological composting without the consumer having to see or even touch the worms.[72] Ecology yes, but without inconvenience, without sacrifice and without changing one's way of life, to quote Jaspers.[73] The 'green' trend must be in line with the modern 'smart tech' trend; products must be 'attractive' to consumers in terms of current market trends and enable producers to make high profits. The 'green' image is merely a marketing strategy to ease guilty consciences and generate even higher profits. In this sense, one can speak of an immoral complicity

[65] Koenig (2023).

[66] Cf. ibid., p. 21.

[67] Cf. ibid., pp. 57 and 80.

[68] Cf. ibid., p. 58.

[69] Cf. ibid., p. 104.

[70] Cf. ibid., p. 62.

[71] Cf. ibid., pp. 131–134.

[72] Cf. ibid., p. 174.

[73] Cf. Jaspers (1987), p. 51.

between financiers, producers and consumers, whereby the actions of individual consumers lead to the failure of serious environmental measures, as do the ethically irresponsible profit-oriented decisions of banks and companies.

In *Humus* comes clearly to the fore Jorge Viñuales grief that the law did and still does not prevent the Anthropocene.[74] Not only collectives—banks, companies, consumers—are portrayed as irresponsible, but also individuals who, collectively, through their actions, to quote Cripps and Bartmann, contribute to the deterioration of the environmental situation where improvements would be possible.[75]

Koenig illustrates the extent of human irresponsibility using the example of the novel's character Philippine, who draws Kevin into a large-scale environmental fraud to obtain six-digit financing. Kevin's worm composter project is promising—insofar as the legal obligation to separate waste will come into force in two years.[76] While Kevin is sincerely convinced of his idea that worms can make waste disposal environmentally friendly and continues to refine his technical concept, Philippine is not interested in worms; she is even vermiphobic[77] and only interested in the promising profit opportunities under the guise of environmental protection.

Thanks to her upper-class background, she has connections to the L'Oréal conglomerate, which is the first to agree to finance industrial worm composting, operating under the name *Veritas*.[78] The advertising slogan is: "Today's worms are tomorrow's truth".[79] In the USA, Philippine succeeds in securing financing from the *Sequoia* investment fund, whose director is convinced that the future lies in agriculture and fertile soil.[80] The funding commitments are tied to minimum quantities of composted waste by worms, which *Veritas* cannot meet on time. To overcome this obstacle, Philippine stages a scam without telling Kevin: Only a third of the waste is composted by the worms, while the other two thirds are taken to the Thiverval waste incineration plant, which emits one tonne of $CO2$ per tonne of waste.[81]

This not only addresses ethical misconduct due to unscrupulous greed, but also criminal fraud against the investors and Kevin himself, who was not informed about these machinations. However, Kevin is guilty of a lack of diligence, as he, as the owner of the company, should have investigated his suspicions of irregularities instead of basking in passive 'ignorance'.[82] Koenig outlines here, on the one hand, the unscrupulous irresponsibility of economic actors whose greed for profit continues to prevent effective mitigation of global warming and, on the other hand, the

[74] Cf. Viñuales (2016), p. 21.
[75] Cf. Cripps (2013), p. 69; Bartmann (2024), pp. 128–129.
[76] Cf. Koenig (2023), p. 142.
[77] Cf. ibid., pp. 172–173.
[78] Cf. ibid., p. 167.
[79] Ibid.
[80] Cf. ibid., p. 223.
[81] Cf. ibid., pp. 396–398.
[82] Cf. ibid., pp. 396–397.

silent complicity of those who could know and act but do not do so out of convenience.

While Kevin rises and falls as a big businessman in the capitalist system in 'green clothing', Arthur consciously opts out of this system and devotes himself unsuccessfully[83] to saving the land left to him by his grandfather. He fights in vain in court against his neighbour Jobard, who continues to practise environmentally harmful agriculture and sues him over a newly planted hedge. How could humans be so stupid, Arthur wonders, as to destroy billions of earthworms that are so important for soil fertility? This is nothing less than "ecocide: the irreparable destruction of an ecosystem by human hands".[84] Here, there is a clear call for legal means to prosecute and punish the destruction of the foundations of human life. The bailiff who delivers the writ of summons to Arthur points out in this context that no effective legal instrument has been used so far: "The justice system serves the interests of environmental polluters. The state is destroying the very foundations on which it is based. This society is rotten. It is based on the exploitation of people and nature and will one day be overthrown by humans or destroyed by nature".[85]

The dominance of economic interests overshadows judicial systems, which continue to interpret the principle of preserving the foundations of life in their rulings—even though it is enshrined in the constitution—in the interests of capitalist and political interests, even in the situation of extreme urgency that is ours worldwide. In the following section we will now shift from our focus from private and economic (ir)responsibility to political responsibility for environmental damage.

4.3 Der Eisbär und die Hoffnung auf morgen

In *Der Eisbär und die Hoffnung auf morgen,*[86] John Ironmonger imagines a confrontation between the climate-sceptic politician Monty Causley and the climate-conscious Tom Horsmith. Tom has lived in the village of St. Pieran since childhood, where Causley owns *Marazion House,* which is located right by the sea and is mostly rented out to tourists.[87] Tom accuses the politician in front of the pub patrons of telling a big lie, namely the lie about climate change, while Benny Shaunessy films the scene with his mobile phone and posts it online:[88] "'I'm just interested in the *one big lie* they're telling people. The biggest lie of all. […] You're a climate denier, Mr. Causley! […] You deny climate change.[…]'".[89] Angered by Causley's

[83] Cf. ibid., p. 192.

[84] Ibid., p. 241.

[85] Ibid., p. 194.

[86] Ironmonger (2024).

[87] Cf. ibid., pp. 17–18.

[88] Cf. ibid., pp. 49–50.

[89] Ibid., p. 43.

refusal to acknowledge the climate-induced rise in sea levels that will soon reach his house, Tom bets that in fifty years the flood will have reached the living room of Causley's house.[90] The circulation of the video on social media brings Tom unwanted fame and damages Causley's political career, who now must fight for credibility after demonstrating how little factual knowledge he has about climate change. Meanwhile, Tom is married to Greenlandic Danish[91] environmental activist Lykke Noorgard,[92] founder of the environmental organisation *Fondation 1820* and the *Glacier Trust*,[93] and lives with her in Qaanaaq, Greenland. Causley holds the post of Minister for the Environment and Climate,[94] a ministry that has been sidelined. Ironically, he was entrusted with this role thanks to the dissemination of the video in St Pieran's pub,[95] but on condition that he improves his lack of knowledge on climate issues[96] and polishes up his poor image with a new, professionally shot video with Tom in which the bet is to be retracted.[97] To this end, Tom and his family are paid for the trip from Greenland to St Pieran, the staging of the video recording is meticulously prepared by the government team: Tom is secretly given a drug mixed into his drink to ensure that Causley performs better during the debate.[98] The conversation is interrupted by a storm raging outside and the rescue operation in aid of two fishermen in distress. Causley, motivated by political interests, distinguishes himself as Tom's saviour by diving after the fishermen, but Lykke drowns because Tom is unable to come to her aid.[99]

Ironmonger's novel depicts the clash between political unscrupulousness and irresponsibility on the one hand and honest, selfless commitment to combating the consequences of the Anthropocene on the other. Tom's anger, knowledge and honesty clash with the personal, selfish and cowardly vanity of the politician Causley, who is only interested in his own career.[100] The moral obligation not to unnecessarily endanger people's livelihoods, to quote Hansson, disappears behind Causley's cowardice and personal vanity. Tom denounces Causley's political arrogance and irresponsible selfishness: "I hate his politics [...] . His arrogance. [...] His constant hypocrisy. I hate him because he simply drugged me to save his own faltering career. [...] I hate him because he won't admit that he denies climate change, because that would be political suicide [...]".[101]

[90] Cf. ibid., p. 47.

[91] Cf. ibid., p. 135.

[92] Cf. ibid., pp. 75–75.

[93] Cf. ibid., p. 126.

[94] Cf. ibid., p. 84.

[95] Cf. ibid., pp. 84–85.

[96] Cf. ibid., p. 94.

[97] Cf. ibid., p. 121.

[98] Cf. ibid., p. 274.

[99] Cf. ibid., pp. 178–181.

[100] Cf. ibid., p. 341.

[101] Cf. ibid., p. 297.

The irresponsibility of those who have the power to change conditions and prevent disasters and death through their decisions, but who do not use it in their own interests, amounts to at least negligent, if not intentional, homicide. Causley's political unscrupulousness violates the state's obligation under the *Paris Climate Agreement*; it violates the state's obligation to do everything in its power to preserve the foundations for a dignified life. The fact that Causley denies climate change out of cowardice and for career reasons, despite knowing exactly "what this crisis consists of",[102] as Tom bitterly remarks, suggests both ethical irresponsibility and legal misconduct. In this sense, Causley, and with him every politician, must be held accountable for the past, present and/or foreseeable consequences of his or her actions, according to the consequence-based principle of legitimacy.[103]

Responsibility for decision-makers in the Anthropocene means conscious information, weighing up the possible consequences of every decision and having the courage to put self-interest behind the planetary interest in the survival of present and future generations under humane living conditions. Law, ethics and intergenerational justice, as Bartmann reminds us,[104] must guide political action in the Anthropocene, because every mistake, every slip-up has devastating long-term consequences for humanity. And humanity no longer has time for human vanity, cowardice, selfishness and lust for power.

5 Conclusion

Three novels, three discourses on responsibility in the Anthropocene and several suggestions that encourage reflection on legal and ethical issues and obstacles. All three projects share the conviction that the law cannot do without the ethical sensitivity of all actors, whether individual or collective, large or small. This idea arises from the simple fact that the climate catastrophe is global and recognizes no geographical or legal boundaries. Only the moral obligation to save planet Earth can create a common, worldwide basis for action. The law varies from country to country, from nation to nation; at best, one can agree on a concise catalogue of minimum fundamental rights such as the right to life and health. Even a fundamental right to freedom is difficult to achieve on a global level. In this sense, Kiefer's and Koenig's proposals for ecocide can be understood as a suitable criminal offence to protect life and health. However, the exact criteria for characterising this offence have yet to be established. Even Kiefer's proposal to include the right to climate in the constitution is less suitable for a global legal claim to the right to a dignified basis of life. The constitutions and the resulting political and legal systems around the world are too different for the enshrinement of a right to climate to offer reliable legal protection.

[102] Ibid., p. 312.

[103] Cf. Heidbrink (2017), p. 13.

[104] Cf. Bartmann (2024), p. 121.

At the same time, Kiefer clearly points to the global dimension of the climate catastrophe, which makes no distinction between rich and poor countries, between North and South, between democratically and authoritatively governed states. The climate catastrophe transcends all boundaries, whether geographical, political, economic, social, cultural or ideological. Every person on our planet is affected by it; every person, apart from those with pathological conditions, has an innate survival instinct. And this is precisely where the idea of a common, global climate ethic, a globally unifying sense of responsibility for the survival of us all, can come into play. There is no distinction between rich and poor, black and white, educated and uneducated, powerful and powerless, because global warming and its devastating consequences do not care whether it affects a wealthy American business magnate or a beggar in the Indian swamps. The only difference is that, thanks to his wealth, the tycoon may die a little later than the Indian beggar, but in the end, they will both die. The ethical responsibility to do everything in our power to mitigate the climate catastrophe therefore lies, as all three novels show, with everyone, with the individual, with the entrepreneur, with the politician.

With the proposal of the energy pass in *Platz der Engel*, Kiefer introduces considerations on measuring individual contributions to the global CO2 budget. In conjunction with the remaining global CO2 budget, which must not be exceeded if the maximum global warming limit of 2 °C set by the *Paris Climate Agreement* is to be met, the imaginary energy pass offers a possible starting point for practical solutions for determining individual responsibility.

In *Humus*, Koenig shows how everyone can contribute to combating climate change through responsible shopping and consumption: many buyers who approve or disapprove of a particular product can influence what is produced and how.

Similarly, in *Der Eisbär und die Hoffnung auf morgen*, Ironmonger suggests that a climate-conscious electorate can force politicians to rethink their positions. The climate-sceptical Causley would not be environment minister if his party had not been elected.

If individual citizens can achieve little on their own, a collective, global sense of responsibility for their own survival and the survival of all, in the interplay of shared behaviours, actions and decisions, or, to use Jaspers's words, a "shared way of life", can contribute significantly to the urgently needed rethinking in the context of the urgency of the Anthropocene. For, as Jean-Paul Sartre so aptly put it, "each of us is guilty towards everyone, for everyone and for everything",[105] which, to quote Jonas, results in a mutual "fiduciary or custodial responsibility of humankind" to enable present and future generations to live a dignified existence on a liveable Earth.

[105] Sartre (1988), p. 165.

Legal Texts and Decisions

French Constitutional Law No. 2005-205 of 1 March 2005.

Paris Agreement of 12 December 2015: https://unfccc.int/sites/default/files/english_paris_agreement.pdf (accessed on 12 November 2025).

District Court of The Hague, Uitspraak op 9 October 2018 – 200.178.245/01, ECLI:NL: GHDHA:2018:2591; similarly: District Court of The Hague, Judgment of 20 December 2019 – 19/00135, ECLI:NL:HR: 2019:2007, para. 5.7.7.

BVerfG, Beschl. v. 24. 03. 2021 – 1 BvR 2656/18 u. a., ECLI:DE:BVerfG:2021: rs20210324.1bvr265618, Ls. 4.

District Court of The Hague, Judgment of 26 May 2021 – C/09/571932/HA ZA 19-379, ECLI:NL:RBDHA:2021:5337.

BVerfG, Beschl. v. 18. 01. 2022 – 1 BvR 1565/21, 1 BvR 1566/21 u. a., NJW 2022, 844, Rn. 12 ff.

EGMR 09.04.2024 (GK), 53600/20, KlimaSeniorinnen ua/Schweiz.

OLG Hamm, 28.05.2025 – 5 U 15/17. https://dejure.org/dienste/vernetzung/rechtsprechung?Text=5%20U%2015/17#Entscheidung2 (accessed on 17 December 2025).

References

Amos, Maximilian. 2024. 'Historischer' Sieg für 'Klimaseniorinnen'. In *Redaktion beck-aktuell*, 9 April 2024.

Aßländer, Michael S. 2022. Gefangenen-Dilemma. In *Handbuch Wirtschaftsethik*, ed. Michael S. Aßländer. Wiesbaden.

Barrau, Aurélien. 2023. *L'Hypothèse K. La science face à la catastrophe écologique*. Paris: Grasset.

Bartmann, Marius. 2024. Brauchen wir eine neue Ethik für das Anthropozän? Individuelle Verantwortung für kollektive Schäden im Kontext. Des Klimawandels. *Zeitschrift für Praktische Philosophie* 11 (2): 119–146.

Bartmann, Marius, and Aurélie Halsband. 2023. Climate Justice: Ethical Aspects. In *Climate Justice. Ethical Aspects and Policy Aspects*, ed. Dirk Lanzerath et al., 13–88. Baden-Baden: Nomos.

Bazargan-Forward, Saba, and Deborah Tollefsen, eds. 2020. *The Routledge Handbook of Collective Responsibility*. New York: Routledge.

Birnbacher, Dieter. 2012. Schwerpunkt: Der Klimawandel und sein Folgen – eine Herausforderung für die Angewandte Ethik. *Jahrbuch für Wissenschaft und Ethik* 16 (1): 89–94.

Birnbacher, Dieter. 2015. Klimagerechtigkeit – Verursacher oder Leistungsfähigkeitsprinzip? In *Klimagerechtigkeit und Klimaethik*, ed. Angela Kallhoff, 67–80. Berlin: De Gruyter.

Birnbacher, Dieter. 2022. *Klimaethik. Eine Einführung*. Stuttgart: Reclam.

Cripps, Elizabeth. 2013. Climate Change, Collective Harm and Legitimate Coercion. *Critical Review of International Social and Political Philosophy* 14 (2): 171–193.

Crutzen, Paul J., and Eugene F. Stormer. 2000. The Anthropocene. *IGBP-Newsletter* 41.

Dürbeck, Gabriele. 2018. Das Anthropozän erzählen: Fünf Narrative. *Aus Politik und Zeitgeschichte: Klima* 21–23:11–17.

Frenz, Walter. 2023. *Grundzüge des Klimaschutzrechts*. 3rd ed. Berlin: Erich Schmidt Verlag.

Hahn, Henning, and Jens Schnitker. 2017. Kollektive Verantwortung in der globalen Ethik. *Zeitschrift für Praktische Philosophie* 4 (1): 109–122.

Hansson, Sven O. 2007. Risk and Ethics: Three Approaches. In *Risk: Philosophical Perspectives*, ed. Tim Lewens, 21–35. London/New York: Routledge.

Heidbrink, Ludger. 2017. Definitionen und Voraussetzungen der Verantwortung. In *Handbuch Verantwortung*, ed. Ludger Heidbrink et al., 3–33. Wiesbaden: Springer.

Honnacker, Ana. 2021. Von Klimasünden, Flugscham, und Moralischen Streckübungen: Ökologisches (Schuld-) Bewusstsein im Anthropozän. *The Germanic Review: Literature, Culture, Theory* 96 (2): 143–158.

Horn, Eva, and Hannes Bergthaller. 2019. *Anthropozän zur Einführung*. Hamburg: Junius.

Ironmonger, John. 2024. *Der Eisbär und die Hoffnung auf morgen*. Berlin: Fischer.

Jaspers, Karl. 1987 [1946]. *Die Schuldfrage. Zur politischen Haftung Deutschlands*. München: Piper.

Jonas, Hans. 1979. *Das Prinzip Verantwortung. Versuch einer Ethik für die technologische Zivilisation*. Frankfurt am Main: Suhrkamp.

Juster, Alexandra. 2025. *Law, Literature and Legal Counterfactuals. A Method of Contrastive Discourse Analysis Using the Example of Contemporary Literature*. Cham: Springer.

Keij, Daan, and Boris R. van Meurs. 2023. Responsibility for Future Climate Justice: The Direct Responsibility to Mitigate Structural Injustice for Future Generations. *Journal of Applied Philosophy* 40 (4): 642–657.

Keller, Reiner. 2018. Diskurs/Diskurstheorien. In *Handbuch Wissenssoziologie und Wissensforschung*, ed. Rainer Schützeichel, 199–213. Cologne: Halem.

Kiefer, Gabriele. 2019. *Platz der Engel*. Zweitausendeins.

Koenig, Gaspar. 2023. *Humus*. Paris: J'ai lu.

Konersmann, Ralf. 2021. Der Philosoph mit der Maske. Michel Foucaults *L'ordre du discours*. In *Die Ordnung des Diskurses*, ed. Michel Foucault, 53–91. Frankfurt am Main: Fischer.

Kruip, Gerhard. 2020. Verantwortung im Anthropozän. *Vierteljahresschrift für wissenschaftliche Pädagogik* 96:25–40.

Lenk, Hans. 2021. Das Prinzip Verantwortung: Systemverantwortung. In *Hans Jonas Handbuch. Leben – Werk – Wirkung*, ed. Michael Bongardt et al. Berlin: J. B. Metzler.

Magnason, Andri S. 2020. *Wasser und Zeit: Eine Geschichte unserer Zukunft*. Berlin: Insel.

Parfit, Derek. 1986. *Reasons and Persons*. Oxford: Oxford University Press.

Roser, Dominic, and Christian Seidel. 2015. *Ethik des Klimawandels: Eine Einführung*. Darmstadt: WBG.

Sartre, Jean-Paul. 1988. Brief an Simone de Beauvoir vom 10. April 1940. In *Jean-Paul Sartre. Briefe an Simone de Beauvoir und andere*, vol. 2. Reinbek bei Hamburg: Rowohlt.

Schneidewind, Uwe. 2018. *Die Große Transformation. Eine Einführung in die Kunst gesellschaftlichen Wandels*. Frankfurt am Main: Fischer Verlag.

Sinder, Rinke. 2021. Anthropozänes Verfassungsrecht als Antwort auf den anthropogenen Klimawandel. Besprechung von BVerfG, Beschl. v. 24. 03. 2021 – 1 BvR 2656/18 u. a. *JuristenZeitung (JZ)* 22:1078–1086.

Skidelsky, Robert, and Edward Skidelsky. 2012. *Wie viel ist genug? Vom Wachstumswahn zu einer Ökonomie des guten Lebens*. München: Wilhelm Goldmann.

Sloterdijk, Peter. 2015. Das Anthropozän – Ein Prozeß-Zustand am Rande der Erd-Geschichte. *Das Anthropozän. Zum Stand der Dinge*25–44.

Steffen, Will, et al. 2015. The Trajectory of the Anthropocene: The Great Acceleration. *The Anthropocene Review* 2 (1): 81–98.

Viñuales, Jorge. 2016. Law and the Anthropocene. *C-EENRG Working Paper* 2016-4. https://papers.ssrn.com/sol3/papers.cfm?abstract_id=2842546 (accessed on 12 September 2025)

Wackernagel, Mathis, and Bert Beyers. 2016. *Footprint. Die Welt neu vermessen*. Hamburg: CEP Europäische Verlagsanstalt.

Wallenhorst, Nathanaël. 2024. Einführung in das Anthropozän. In *Nathanaël Wallenhorst: Eine kritische Theorie für das Anthropozän*, 73–91. Wiesbaden: Springer.

Wallimann-Helmer, Ivo. 2017. Kollektive Verantwortung für den Klimaschutz. *Zeitschrift für Praktische Philosophie* 4 (1): 211–238.

Wissenschaftlicher Beirat der Bundesregierung Globale Umweltveränderungen (WBGU). 2011. *Hauptgutachten: Welt im Wandel. Gesellschaftsvertrag für eine Große Transformation*. Berlin, https://www.wbgu.de/fileadmin/user_upload/wbgu/publikationen/hauptgutachten/hg2011/pdf/wbgu_jg2011.pdf (accessed on 13 November 2025).

Jean Giono's *The Man Who Planted Trees*: Critical Nature Writing, *Enlivement*, and Humans as Trustees of Nature

Alexandra Juster

Abstract Jean Giono's short eco-critical story *The Man Who Planted Trees* anticipates the current debates since its publication in 1953 in the well-advanced Anthropocene era concerning the human causes of nature's destruction and the interactions between nature and culture. Questioning the anthropocentric worldview of Western society, it attempts to offer a biocentric counter-narrative that informs twenty-first-century socio-cultural and legal reflections. Giono's biocentric counter-model bears a striking resemblance to indigenous legal systems and worldviews, as evidenced by the Ecuadorian Constitution of 2008. Following a brief introduction to the emergence of the concept of 'critical nature writing' in recent German literary studies, an insight into legal considerations regarding the relationship between legal subjects (humans/nature) and legal objects (nature) will be provided. The analysis of Giono's story *The Man Who Planted Trees* will consider both literary approaches to critical 'nature writing' and contemporary legal perspectives on nature rights.

Keywords Jean Giono · Anthropocene · Critical nature writing · Nature rights · Anthropocentrism · Biocentrism

In 1953, Jean Giono wrote a very short story entitled *The Man Who Planted Trees*.[1] In the English-speaking world, it could be classified as belonging to the literary genre of *ecocriticism*. In German-language literature, it would be classified as part of the emerging trend of 'critical nature writing'. In just a few pages, it presciently raises the big questions that dominate and animate current debates in the context of the (too) advanced Anthropocene. They concern the causes of climate change and

[1] In the original version, *L'homme qui plantait des arbres*.

A. Juster (✉)
University of Innsbruck, Innsbruck, Austria
e-mail: Alexandra.Juster@uibk.ac.at

A. Juster (ed.), *Legal Drafts in Anthropocene Literature*, SpringerBriefs in Law,
https://doi.org/10.1007/978-3-032-27283-6_3

its anticipated devastating effects on human and non-human life on planet Earth. They concern the Western, anthropocentric worldview that considers itself superior to nature as an exploitable resource, as well as its destructive consequences. They concern the individual and collective responsibility of today and tomorrow. All these issues are illustrated through the narrative in *The Man Who Planted Trees*, focusing on the central character of Elzéard Bouffier. He seems to pioneer the currently widely discussed idea of granting rights to the non-human beings. Nature should be recognised as a legal subject to defend its rights and counteract its destruction.

Before moving on to an interdisciplinary analysis of this pioneering idea of nature rights in Giono's short story, I will first discuss the literary concept of 'critical nature writing' and the current legal debates on the rights of nature. In the third and final part, the study of *The Man Who Planted Trees* will focus on the destruction of nature and culture, its causes, and possible regeneration. It will also consider the legal concept of collective fiduciary responsibility, which stems from the idea of nature being granted legal personhood and thus becoming a rights-bearing entity.

1 'Critical Nature Writing' and Ruined Nature

While German critical nature writing developed less dynamically than Anglophone ecocriticism until a few years ago, Elisabeth Weydt points out that Alexander von Humboldt, however, recognised and noted the human impact on nature as early as the eighteenth century.[2] In this context, Caroline Schumann emphasises Humboldt's holistic understanding of the connections and interactions in the biosystem as well as his "systems thinking, which regards human action as part of the ecosystem".[3] Both ideas are considered in today's ecological debates. During his five-year journey through South America, von Humboldt observed the devastating effects of the Spanish colonisers on the South American environment: "But the Spaniards treated the water as an enemy. They apparently want this New Spain to be as dry as the interior districts of their old Spain. They want nature to resemble their morals, and they are not doing badly in this regard […]".[4] The fact that 'nature writing' for him is not merely a romantic description of nature, but is intended to stimulate critical reflection, becomes clear in the following passage from his writings: "Philosophical natural history rises above the needs of a mere description of nature. It does not consist of a sterile accumulation of facts".[5]

After this early German 'interlude', we return to Anglophone *ecocriticism*: in 1949, Aldo Leopold's *A Sand County Almanac* (1949) was published in the United

---

[2] Cf. Weydt (2023), p. 244.

[3] Schaumann (2024), p. 37; all the translations into English are mine.

[4] von Humboldt (2003), p. 254.

[5] von Humboldt (1849), II, p. 289.

States. In it, the American forester, professor and philosopher, who had died the year before, criticises the anthropocentric worldview of human ownership of nature: "Critics write and hunters outwit their game primarily for one and the same reason – to reduce that beauty to possession".[6] Leopold warns presciently against the destruction of nature through economic exploitation: "Land-use ethics are still governed wholly by economic self-interest […]".[7] As Axel Goodbody explains, the *ecocriticism* movement began in the United States in the late 1960s, when the environmental movement reached its peak.[8] William Rueckert was one of the first to coin the term *ecocriticism* as "the application of ecology and ecological concepts to the study of literature".[9] The *Association for the Study of Literature and Environment* (ASLE), founded in 1992, marks the beginning of this new phase of *ecocriticism*. It describes its mission in the following words: "to promote the exchange of ideas and information about literature and other cultural representations that consider human relationships with the natural world".[10] Soon, as Goodbody goes on to explain, studies on Henry David Thoreau and other literary works from an ecological perspective appeared.[11] In 1996, Cheryll Glotfelty and Harold Fromm published the groundbreaking, comprehensive volume *Ecocriticism Reader: Landmarks in Literary Ecology*, with analyses of the interrelationships between literature and ecology.[12] The fact that the understanding of this literary approach has changed since then becomes clear in Cheryll Glotfelty's work. She defines the term '*ecocriticism*' as "the study of the relationship between literature and the physical environment",[13] although the essential observation of human agency was not yet in focus. According to Goodbody, Jonathan Bate's *Romantic Ecology. Wordsworth and the Environmental Tradition* (1991) was the first study in Great Britain to take a decidedly ecocritical approach.[14] This was followed a few years later by Lawrence Buell's *The Environmental Imagination. Thoreau, Nature Writing and the Formation of American Culture* (1995).[15] However, as Goodbody critically notes in 2007, Anglo--American *ecocriticism* has not yet arrived in Germany. This is certainly attributable to the technocratic understanding of dominance over all natural processes and the unpleasant connotations of the concept of homeland due to its ideological instrumentalization in National Socialism.

Despite all the criticism, Hubert Zapf's cultural-ecological approaches should not be ignored either. These prompt him, in line with Goodbody's negative

[6] Leopold (1971), p. 230.

[7] Ibid., p. 245.

[8] Cf. Goodbody (2007b).

[9] Glotfelty and Fromm (1996), p. xx.

[10] Goodbody (2007a), p. 8.

[11] Cf. ibid., p. 7.

[12] Cf. Glotfelty and Fromm (1996).

[13] Ibid., p. xxxi.

[14] Cf. Goodbody (2007a), p. 8; Bate (1991).

[15] 15 Buell (1995)

assessment, to examine literature according to ecocritical criteria—with specific reference to American *ecocriticism*: "The nonhuman environment is present not merely as a framing device but as a presence that begins to suggest that human history is implicated in natural history".[16]

Since then, a new, critically oriented trend in *nature writing* has been developing in German-language literary research for several years. Christine Kanz labels this as "critical *nature* writing",[17] distinguishing it from both Anglo-American *ecocriticism* and the nature poetry of German Romanticism. Ludwig Fischer's definitional considerations on new *nature writing*, which he traces back to the "intensive [...] exploration of concrete nature and landscape", has autobiographical features, meets high aesthetic standards and—of particular interest to us—contains an emotionally charged "protest energy" in the form of "counter-narratives".[18] Jürgen Goldstein sees this form of writing as a particularly attentive attitude on the part of the author towards the "visible but overlooked",[19] which, however, is only constituted through precise language and the naming of the non-human.[20] Against the backdrop of the current environmental catastrophe, all these theoretical concepts share the awareness that literature has an ethical responsibility to convey.[21]

In France, philosophers such as Michel Serres, Gaston Bachelard, Pierre Hadot, Félix Guattari and Catherine Larrère, anthropologists such as Philippe Descola, and sociologists such as Roger Caillois and Bruno Latour have been and continue to engage with the problematic dialectic of culture and nature.[22] In this context, Nathalie Blanc, Thomas Pughe and Denis Chartier emphasise the political character of French *écocritique*, which seeks to inspire action through literature and art.[23] The strong networking among scholars who feel affiliated with this field testifies to its political orientation. Choné cites as an example the *ZoneZadir* collective, founded in 2018 by literary scholars, whose name alludes to the acronym 'ZAD' (*zone à* défendre/defence zone).[24] In recent years, a new generation of eco-critical writers, lawyers and artists has been emerging in France, including Erik Orsenna,[25] Baptiste Morizot and Suzanne Husky,[26] Camille de Toledo[27] and Pascal Nicolas-Le Strat.[28] They do not limit themselves to a critical reading of the relationship between

[16] Zapf (2008), p. 855; cf. Zapf (2002).

[17] Kanz (2023), p. 42.

[18] Fischer (2019), pp. 45–47 and 58–59; cf. Kanz (2023), p. 31.

[19] Goldstein (2018), p. 104; cf. Kanz (2023), p. 31.

[20] Cf. Goldstein (2019), pp. 26–27.

[21] Cf. Kanz (2023), pp. 43–44.

[22] Cf. Choné (2019), p. 327.

[23] Cf. Blanc et al. (2008).

[24] Cf. Choné (2019), p. 328.

[25] Cf. Orsenna (2025).

[26] Cf. Morizot and Husky (2024).

[27] Cf. de Toledo (2021).

[28] Cf. Nicolas-Le Strat (2018).

humans and nature, but also urgently call for action against the climate catastrophe. They illustrate the progressive destruction of the environment in narrative, visual or theatrical form and advocate for the recognition of non-humans as legal subjects equal to humans.

The destructive effects of human activity on planet Earth (destruction of nature and species, depletion of resources, pollution, littering, etc.), which have been critically denounced by intellectuals, leave behind ruins and ruined landscapes. Jens Soentgen describes these as "fractal structures".[29] They reveal the rupture between nature and culture in its spatial and temporal dimensions.[30] According to Auerochs, the "ruin" tells the viewer that something is missing.[31] Georg Simmel understands it as a "site of (cultural, author's note) life from which life has departed".[32] From the perspective of the "ethos of enlivenment",[33] however, dead spaces in the cultural sense, populated by building and industrial ruins, can be revived through ecological *enlivenment*. This concept of revitalisation through 'ecologization' is particularly relevant in the context of the Anthropocene, which is inextricably linked to the theme of (survival) life. It considers the interdependence and interactions between the human and the non-human. Hildegard Kurt and Andreas Weber understand this space as a space of poietic vitality, in which dead resources are revived by new forms of life.[34] Anna Tsing aptly formulates this idea: "Although they have been declared dead, they can still show signs of life; areas that have been abandoned sometimes give rise to new species-rich and multicultural life".[35] The concept of 'enlivement' thus signals hope; it leaves open the possibility of restoration and survival if mankind takes the right actions to make this resurrection possible.

As will be demonstrated in the last section, Jean Giono's short story *The Man Who Planted Trees*, written over seventy years ago, anticipates Kanz's 'critical nature writing' and Kurt and Weber's concept of ecological *enlivenment*, conveying a message of faith in humanity's capacity to restore nature and its fundamentals of life.

In the following section, a legal-theoretical discussion of the concepts of nature rights and humans as 'trustees' of nature in a biocentric self-image will precede the actual analysis of the story. Giono already clearly anticipated these concepts in *The Man Who Planted Trees,* which are driving today's legal debates with increased, if not feverish, intensity in view of mildening the effects of the Anthropocene.

---

[29] Soentgen (1997), p. 126.

[30] Cf. Auerochs (2022), p. 88.

[31] Ibid., p. 93.

[32] Simmel (1919), p. 132.

[33] Kurt and Weber (2015), p. 11.

[34] Cf. Kurt and Weber (2015), p. 12; Auerochs (2022), p. 94.

[35] Tsing (2019), p. 20.

2 On the Debate About Nature Rights and the 'Trustee' Function of Humans

Society, its understanding of law and the position of humans in our world are closely interlinked. Law as a social phenomenon supports the world view of those who created it. In this sense, the industrialised Western world and its legal systems are anthropocentric, focusing on humans as 'owners' and as the natural, self-evident legal subjects. It inherits Descartes' rational anthropocentric worldview—*'cogito, ergo sum'*—in which humans are elevated to masters of nature.[36] In line with the capitalist orientation of society, economically and socially relevant 'entities' such as companies, associations, cooperatives, etc. are 'artificially' granted legal personality. Depending on the needs, obligations are imposed on humans vis-à-vis other humans or non-humans, or limits are set. In Western culture, however, nature, air, water, rivers, lakes, seas, mountains, glaciers, etc. are not treated as ipso facto *natural legal entities*. They are not legal entities 'in their own right'. Attributing the ability to possess and enforce rights to non-human entities contradicts the anthropocentric vision according to which only humans possess rights and can enforce them in court (*agency*). Only humans can claim property rights, including over the non-human,[37] humans do not see themselves as an integral part of their environment, but as its owners, separate from it and superior to it. This anthropocentric attitude leads to the exploitation of natural resources in the service of a never-ending capitalist race that fears one thing above all else: economic recession, the decline in profits in the name of the 'value' of material enrichment and the social recognition that comes with this accumulated material wealth. Such a scale of values is alien to the idea of giving space to values other than those of economic, quantifiable wealth—in contrast to some indigenous cultures, such as those still existing in South America and the Pacific region. We will return to this in more detail in the following chapter. For generations, they have been informed by a biocentric conception of life and have lived in harmony with their natural environment. Their model of society and values could help to reposition nature and non-humans within Western capitalist structures, thereby hindering environmental destruction and the resulting self-destruction of humanity. However, as Vincent Hoppmann critically notes, scientific engagement with the legal systems of the Global South still seems to be relatively uncommon in the Global North,[38] due to the difficulty of achieving social acceptance of the radical shift in thinking from anthropocentrism to biocentrism.

Warnings and considerations on how to halt anthropogenic destruction of the world date back to the second half of the twentieth century. As already mentioned, Aldo Leopold criticised the anthropocentric world view of human ownership of nature in his book *A Sand County Almanac*.[39] The defensive idea of granting nature

---

[36] Cf. Descartes (1637).

[37] Cf. Wesche (2023).

[38] Cf. Hoppmann (2025), pp. 443–444.

[39] Cf. Leopold (1971), p. 245.

its own rights was first taken up by Clarence Morris in 1964,[40] before Christopher D. Stone formulated it in his much-discussed 1972 article "Should Trees Have Standing".[41] Norwegian philosopher Arne Næss advocates for biocentric thinking that recognises the intrinsic value of nature.[42] In France, Marie-Angèle Hermitte was the first to propose the idea of nature as a legal entity.[43] Michel Serres developed the concept of the 'contract with nature' (*contrat naturel*)—derived from Rousseau's *contrat* social.[44] Thomas Berry is considered the founder of *Earth Jurisprudence* (*Earth Law*), which demands legal subject status for non-humans.[45]

At the international level, the *UN World Charter for Nature,* proclaimed in 1982, commits itself for the first time to a biocentric worldview: "Mankind is a part of nature and life […]." The *Earth Charter,* proclaimed in 2000, conveys the biocentric idea even more clearly: "Earth is our home, is alive with a unique community of life." Article 25 of *the United Nations Declaration on the Rights of Indigenous Peoples* of 2007 supplements the *Earth Charter* with spiritual values, based on the holistic worldview of indigenous cultures: "Indigenous peoples have the right to maintain and strengthen their distinctive spiritual relationship with their traditionally owned or otherwise occupied and used lands, territories, waters and coastal seas and other resources […]." This implicitly results in a recognition of the knowledge of indigenous peoples and their role as qualified 'stewards' of nature in the sense of Hans Jonas' "stewardship or stewardship responsibility of humankind": In view of the global challenges of climate change, the concept of responsibility for humans must be expanded from the individual polluter pay principle to a present and future-oriented trustee principle that includes the idea of collective responsibility.[46] According to this vision, nature and the non-human need to be considered as 'commons' that belong to everyone and no one in particular. Everybody is therefore responsible for preserving the non-human world. Since the non-human cannot defend its own rights in court, humankind is also entrusted with what Jonas calls 'stewardship' of the non-human, i.e. its protection and defence if necessary.

While the majority of current debates on the Anthropocene discuss the relationship between humans and nature maintaining the difference between the human and the non-human, "many indigenous peoples", as Tina Rametsteiner points out, "see themselves as part of nature and the world as a coherent whole in which no part has the right to dominate another part".[47] Similarly, the Western understanding of the term 'rights of nature' in the sense of legislation or jurisprudence that grants rights to nature or to parts of it diverges from the holistic character of certain indigenous

[40] Cf. Morris (1964), pp. 189–190.

[41] Cf. Stone (1972).

[42] Cf. Næss (1972); Routley (1973), pp. 205–210.

[43] Cf. Hermitte (1988); Hermitte (2011); Hermitte (2023).

[44] Cf. Serres (1990).

[45] Cf. Berry (2006), p. 96.

[46] Cf. Lenk (2021), pp. 140–141.

[47] Rametsteiner (2025), p. 32.

cultures.[48] For them, the concept of the cosmos and the world—the 'nurturing Mother Earth', of which they consider themselves as integral part—extends beyond the Western notion of 'rights of nature'.[49] As Elisabeth Weydt explains, the Andean peoples combine spiritual and physical elements in their biocentric worldview, which they refer to with different variations of the term *Pachamama*: "Pacha originates from the languages […] of the great peoples of the Andes. It means […] universe perhaps, a force, a source […]. Pacha thus stands for everything, for the totality of being, for a balance between opposites […]. There is no outside of nature, everything is nature, including humans".[50] For them, nature is the basis for the possibility of leading a "good life, i.e. a life in harmony – *sumak kawsay* – with *Mamapacha*".[51] This concept refers to the harmonious and respectful coexistence of humans with all elements of the cosmos—the *Pachmama*[52]– which is different from the Western pursuit of a materially richer and better life. The enshrinement of these Andean nature rights alongside *sumak kawsay* in a traditional legal institution such as the Ecuadorian Constitution of 2008 has, to date, triggered numerous initiatives aimed at protecting nature through legal instruments. However, Ecuador is the only country so far to have granted *Pachamama* fundamental rights at constitutional level. Indeed, article 71 of the Ecuadorian Constitution therefore states: "Nature, or Pachamama, where life reproduces and realises itself, has the right to have its existence, as well as the preservation and regeneration of its life cycles […], its structure, function and evolutionary processes respected in an integral manner".[53]

In other countries, such as in New Zealand, the *Te Urewera* forest area and the *Te Awa Tupua* River have been granted legal personality, as have the *Arato* river and the Amazon region in Colombia. In Bolivia the *Via Parque Isla de Salamanca* national park and 'Mother Earth' have been declared legal entities. In the USA, Lake Erie and several rivers, as well as the *Manoomin* wild rice variety, have been granted legal personality.[54] In India, the High Court declared the *Ganges* and *Yamuna* rivers and the surrounding glacier regions to be legal entities.[55] In other countries, rivers have been declared legal entities or at least worthy of protection: in Bangladesh (*Turag* River), Australia (*Yarra* River), and Canada (*Magpie River*). In Peru, besides Marañón River, Lake Titicaca was very recently declared a legal

[48] Cf. ibid., pp. 33–34.

[49] Cf. Gomez-Muller (2024), pp. 9, 54 and 75.

[50] Weydt (2023), p. 75.

[51] Weydt (2023), p. 2; cf. Gomez-Muller (2024), p. 31; Rametsteiner (2025), pp. 117–118; Nelson and Shilling (2018).

[52] Cf. Gomez-Muller (2024), pp. 31–34.

[53] Knauβ (2020), p. 225.

[54] Cf. Rametsteiner (2025), pp. 316–317; Pelizzon (2025), pp. 220–231.

[55] Cf. Pelizzon (2025), pp. 231–232.

entity.[56] In Europe, the *Mar Menor* ecosystem in Spain was declared a legal entity with its own rights for the first time in 2022.[57]

The interlinked concepts of *Pachamama* and *sumak kawsay* (*buen vivir* in Quechua), which have found their way into the Ecuadorian Constitution, are of particular interest for a 'recalibration' of both society's orientation towards life in the sense of Bruno Latour's dissolution of the dividing lines between nature and culture[58] and the legal system. Like Latour, Arturo Escobar, Philppe Descola and Catherine Larrère attribute the ecological crisis to the rational dualism between culture and nature.[59] Olivier Barrière et al. refer—under the term *coviability*—to the interdependence between all living human and non-human organisms and entities, which also gives rise to mutual responsibility.[60] This refers to the concept of ecological solidarity within a community of subjects composed of humans and non--humans, in which the boundary between the subject 'human' and the object 'non-human' dissolves. There are mutual relationships and connections (*liens de viabilité*) between all components of this 'community' that link the human with the non-human, just as a social group can be connected to a river, a forest or a lake.[61] Considerations on how to incorporate these reciprocal interrelationships between 'subjects' rather than between 'subjects' and 'objects' into a legal system[62] include the so-called *Traditional Ecological Knowledge* (TEK), i.e. the holistic worldview and knowledge of indigenous peoples.[63] In his latest reflections, Alexandre Zabalza proposes separating legal subject and legal personality: for while only humans can enjoy rights (legal subject) and enforce them in court, non-humans can certainly enjoy rights (legal subject) but cannot actively defend them (legal personality). To do so, they lack the *agency* that only humans can provide. In this sense, Zabalza proposes a separation between legal subject and legal personality for non-humans: non-humans should only be granted legal subjectivity. On the other hand, the lack of legal personality should be supplemented by the duty of care owed by humans, i.e. the above-mentioned stewardship, to ensure mutual viability (*liens de viabilité*).[64] The Ecuadorian Constitution and Article 6 of the Spanish *Mar Menor* law already grant humans such a right of care. Under the concept of *actio popularis*, this grants

[56] Cf. Liendo Tagle (2025).

[57] Cf. Pelizzon (2025), pp. 234–238.

[58] Cf. Latour (2020).

[59] Cf. Escobar (2018), p. 140; Descola (2005); Larrère (2015).

[60] Cf. Barrière et al. (2019); Michelot (2022); Barrière (2022); Camproux Duffrène (2022).

[61] Cf. Barrière (2022), p. 9.

[62] Cf. Latour (2020).

[63] 'TEK' stands for the traditional ecological knowledge that indigenous peoples have acquired through their direct contact with nature over generations about their environment, plants, animals, natural phenomena and everything living and non-living. TEK stands for a spiritual, biocentric philosophy of life that sees humans as an integral part of nature, in the broader sense of our concept of 'nature'.

[64] Cf. Zabalza (2025), pp. 198–199.

humans the possibility of enforcing the rights of non-humans in court.[65] Zabalza therefore proposes extending this right under the term *actio popularis naturalis* to protect the collective (and no longer individual) common good of the 'environment'.[66] This would mean that anyone is entitled to act in court to defend the non-human.

The following section will discuss more in detail the philosophical and legal considerations regarding a possible biocentric vision of nature and the non-human as legal subjects, as well as the function of humans as trustees, guardians and caretakers of the non-human to protect its rights, which were anticipated as early as 1953 in Jean Giono's short story *The Man Who Planted Trees.*

3 Analysis of Jean Giono's *The Man Who Planted Trees*

Jean Giono was born on 30 March 1895 in Manosque in the southern French Alps. In the interwar period of the 1930s, he published several works: *Second Harvest* (1930), *The Solitude of Compassion* (1932), *The Serpent of Stars* (1937), *The Song of the World* (1937), and *Joy of Man's Desiring* (1940). This established him as a well-known writer. His career suffered a setback when, at the end of the Second World War, he was accused of complicity with Nazi Germany and imprisoned. In addition, his works were blacklisted in 1945. Giono's 'return' to the public eye in 1948 with the two novels *A King without Diversion* (1947) and *Noé* (1947) reveals a 'new' Giono, who in his writings turns his attention less to people and more to the natural landscape.[67]

Peter Mortensen categorises Giono's story *The Man Who Planted Trees*[68] without hesitation as ecocritical literature: "Ecocritical interest in Giono has so far primarily centred on his short story 'The Man Who Planted Trees' [...]".[69]

According to Jean-Philippe Pierron, the point here is not so much to celebrate the connection with the landscape as to show the violent reaction of a beautiful nature 'in panic', which is not just the backdrop but the 'living' protagonist of the narrative.[70] In this sense, Gaston Bachelard refers to the political role of literature, which is by no means limited to *l'art pour l'art*: "The poet does not describe; he knows very well that his task is greater than that".[71] Giono himself seems to confirm this

---

[65] Cf. Delzangles and Zabalza (2023), pp. 606–616; Bosselmann (2024).

[66] Cf. Zabalza (2025), pp. 199–201.

[67] Cf. Marion (2020), pp. 30–31.

[68] I refer to the freely accessible electronic version of Jean Giono's *The Man Who Planted Trees*, published by the Indian Friends of Elzéard Bouffier in 1999, Giono (1999). Cf. the electronic link: https://www.arvindguptatoys.com/arvindgupta/manplantedtrees.pdf (accessed on 19 December 2025). The original French version is *L'Homme qui plantait des arbres.*

[69] Mortensen (2017), p. 186.

[70] Cf. Pierron (2012), p. 14.

[71] Bachelard (1983), p. 170.

when he writes in a letter to the conservator of water and forests of Digne in 1957: "I believe it is high time for a tree policy".[72]

Olivier Serrat sees Giono's 'greater task', in Bachelard's sense, as an encouragement to persistently campaign for environmental protection. It does not show an apocalyptic, hopeless end, but rather points to possible solutions through renewal, sustainability and the restoration of the symbiosis between humans and nature.[73]

Giono sets the story in the French Southern Alps between Sisteron and Mirabeau. The area is bordered to the southeast and south by the Durance River, to the north by the upper reaches of the Drôme River, and to the west by the plains of the *Venaissin* county and the foothills of *Mont Ventoux*.[74]

In the mid-nineteenth century, only around 10% of the land surface in this region was still covered by forest. The Southern Alps had been almost completely deforested due to intensive timber consumption for industry, construction and warfare. This resulted in flooding, which encountered no resistance on the bare slopes. In 1856, a particularly serious disaster struck the region, leaving a lasting mark on the territory and its inhabitants and leading to the recognition of the urgent need for reforestation measures. Under Napoleon III, a law on reforestation was enacted in 1860 (*loi du 28 juillet 1860*), with the requirement to 1,100,000 hectares of land to be reforested. The legally mandated reforestation was followed 22 years later by a law on 4 April 1882 for the restoration and conservation of mountain areas. From 1886 onwards, photography was used to visually record the forest stands (see Fig. 1).

In 1863, Prosper Demontzey was appointed curator of the Southern Alps and entrusted with supervising the reforestation work.[75] This geographical and eco-historical background is the setting for Giono's story *The Man Who Planted Trees*.

Elzéard Bouffier[76] decides, after the death of his wife and son, to settle alone in the small mountain village of Vergons as a mountain shepherd[77] and later as a bee-keeper.[78] In addition to his daily work, he collects acorns, selects the hundred best ones and carefully buries them in the ground every day.[79] He continues to do this for many years until his death. Later, he also plants beech and birch trees to better adapt the tree species to the soil.[80] He does not care who ownes the land in which he plants the seeds.[81] We learn this from the story of a lonely wanderer who got lost in 1913

[72] Cit. in Pierron (2012), p. 11.

[73] Cf. Serrat (2025); Citron (1995), p. 9.

[74] Cf. Giono (1999), p. 5.

[75] Cf. Leroux (2024); France Nature Environnement (2025); Focus Agate (2024); Pardé (1998); Cf. https://francearchives.gouv.fr/fr/findingaid/e66bb6fdfc4ab442c397d52d2a6e41b8e0b048d9 (accessed on 1 December 2025).

[76] Giono (1999), p. 16.

[77] Cf. ibid., p. 32.

[78] Cf. ibid., p. 41.

[79] Cf. ibid., p. 12.

[80] Cf. ibid., p. 18.

[81] Cf. ibid., pp. 15–16.

Fig. 1 "Torrent du Bourget (atterrissement du barrage n° 6 et barrages n° 7 à 12, atterrissement du barrage n° 12, barrages n° 1 à 6, vue du torrent et cone de déjection) / Sardi 1887, Gallica / Archives nationales" (Lic. CC0), https://agate.inrae.fr/ark:/12148/btv1b10701277q?rk=107296;4 (accessed on 20 March 2026)

during a hike in the treeless and waterless mountain region.[82] In his anxious search for water, he encounters Elzéard Bouffier, who, without much fuss, provides him with water and food. He visits him repeatedly, interrupted only by the two World Wars, and observes the transformation of the formerly ruined, parched and uninhabitable landscape into '*enlived*' land thanks to Elzéard's unwavering 'tree planting', which he continues even during the war years: by 1945, the land is already reforested and green again, water is bubbling and new inhabitants are settling there. As

[82] Cf. ibid., p. 28.

Gabriele Corsani notes, the setting of the story, Vergons, is once again becoming a beautiful place for communal living thanks to ecological renewal.[83]

In his story, Giono establishes a causal connection between man-made, irresponsible destruction in an anthropocentric worldview and the possibility of 'healing' by the same human hand, if it acts responsibly and fits into a biocentric worldview. Happiness in life can be found not separately from nature, but as part of it.

3.1 Fractal Structures, Absence and Enlivenment

The landscape encountered by the hiker in *The Man Who Planted Trees* presents itself as a fractal structure in the sense of Jens Soentgen, in which nature and culture, the natural and the man-made, lie in ruins. The break between the human and the non-human becomes apparent here: instead of living in harmony with nature in the holistic indigenous understanding of *Mamapacha* and *sumak kawsay*, humans have left the region after disrupting biological cycles through excessive deforestation and continuing their destructive work elsewhere. The effortless abandonment of destroyed nature, which can no longer be exploited, demonstrates, on the one hand, the survival of Descartes' image of man as master and, on the other, man's refusal to recognise the intrinsic value of the non-human in the sense of Næss' concept of *deep ecology.*[84]

The consequence of this irresponsible behaviour is the creation of ruined 'wastelands' dominated by "dryness" and "coarse grasses", from which "all life has vanished".[85] The lonely wanderer has little hope of finding a source of water and fears for his survival: "I had run out of water the day before and had to find some".[86] According to his biographer Andrea Wulf, Alexander von Humboldt had already recognised in the eighteenth century that there is a direct link between intensive deforestation and water shortages: "If you destroy the forests, as European settlers are doing everywhere in America with careless haste, the springs will dry up or at least diminish greatly. The riverbeds lie dry for part of the year and become torrential streams whenever heavy rain falls in the mountains".[87] Humboldt describes here the same phenomena that faced the public forestry administration of the Southern French Alps in the nineteenth century.

The destruction of nature is followed by cultural ruin: as far as the eye can see, "vestiges of an abandoned village [...], clustered houses, [...] five or six houses,

---

[83] Cf. Corsani (2015), p. 17.

[84] According to Naess' concept of 'deep ecology', humans are only part of nature and as such cannot see their needs supersede the general environmental balance. The only way to prevent climate change is a total switch in the human way of life and a drastic reduction in population (cf. Næss 1972).

[85] Giono (1999), pp. 6–7.

[86] Ibid., p. 6.

[87] Cit. in Wulf (2016), p. 39.

roofless, gnawed by wind and rain, the tiny chapel with its crumbling steeple".[88] The wind howls in the "carcasses of the houses".[89] What remains are rare hamlets, mostly those of charcoal burners who live off charcoal. Life there is difficult due to epidemics, strife, suicide and insanity.[90]

Giono already recognises here the causality between the destruction of nature and the occurrence of epidemics, as the Covid-19 epidemic has demonstrated to us with full force in the recent past. With the greedy exploitation of nature, humans are not only destroying their material foundations for life, but also their personal balance and contentment. How can humans find happiness when there is nothing but devastation around them? Giono also points to the potential for conflict between individuals, collectives, regions and states, which we now recognise as an imminent and very worrying challenge. The struggle for resources and for territories that are still worth living in has already begun. In this sense, as early as 1953, Giono denounced the individualistic and selfish philosophy of life that characterises Western industrialised nations and their legal systems today, in contrast to the collective thinking and actions of certain indigenous peoples. He accuses the now ruined village communities of indulging their selfishness delivering a "ceaseless combat between virtue and vice".[91] The choice of the charcoal burner is also no coincidence: with his activity of burning wood, he not only destroys the wood, but also enriches the atmosphere with CO_2 and CO emissions. His activity is emblematic of humanity's potential for destruction when exercised excessively and without regard for the rights of nature.

3.2 Enlivement

As mentioned above, dead resources can be revived by new forms of life. This form of ecological *enlivenment* is clearly present in *The Man Who Planted Trees*. Giono points out that there is only hope for the future if there is a peaceful, harmonious relationship between the human and the non-human, and he anticipates the idea of humans as legal subjects among other legal subjects. If the rights of nature are preserved—in this case through Elzéar's tireless, loving planting of trees—the basis of human life can also be restored and secured. The relationship must be based on mutual respect. If humans recognise their own limits and those of nature as legal entities, it is possible to coexist in a shared whole without a hierarchy between humans as masters and nature as an object of exploitation. Giono thus anticipates the holistic principle of harmony known in the Andean indigenous cultures as *Mamapacha* as well as their concept of *sumak kawsay*, or good living together. For

---

[88] Giono (1999), p. 6.

[89] Ibid., p. 7.

[90] Cf. ibid., p. 12.

[91] Ibid.

the person who first finds his way back to a healthy, peaceful and harmonious life is Elzéard. This is no coincidence, but the result of his efforts to enter into a respectful dialogue with the nature that surrounds him. After restoring a dilapidated house and waterproofing its roof, a return to an orderly life becomes possible: "The place was in order, the dishes washed, the floor swept, the rifle oiled; his soup was boiling over the fire".[92] Elzéard makes a confident impression: "One felt that he was sure of himself, and confident in his assurance".[93] He has no need for the distraction of smoking; he lives in an atmosphere of calm and peace (cf. TMPT 12), in which even the two World Wars pass him by unnoticed:[94] "He's discovered a wonderful way to be happy".[95] He owes his good health to his fulfilling work of planting trees with great dedication and care: of the hundred thousand oak trees he has planted over the past three years, ten thousand have already sprouted[96] and the young forest stretches for kilometres.[97] Where drought and aridity drove people away just a few years ago, water now flows again, testifying to the "most impressive result of chain reaction".[98] In addition to water, there are now also "willows, rushes, meadows, gardens, flowers and a certain purpose in being alive".[99] The creation of a new balance between culture and nature brings back hope and *buen vivir*, *sumak kawsay* or the 'good life' in the indigenous sense:

> Ruins had been cleared away, dilapidated walls torn down and five houses restored. Now there were twenty-eight inhabitants, four of them young married couples. The new houses, freshly plastered, were surrounded by gardens where vegetables and flowers grew in orderly confusion, cabbages and roses, leeks and snapdragons, celery and anemones. It was now a village where one would like to live.[100]

With linguistic power, Giono contrasts the sad, gloomy and hopeless existence of people who do not respect the nature's—to quote the Ecuadorian Constitution—"preservation and regeneration [...] life cycles [...], structure, function and evolutionary processes [...] in an integral manner".[101] Everything in our cosmos, in our world, on our 'Mother Earth', including nature, is, in the indigenous understanding, interaction and harmony. If the latter is disturbed, the basis of life is seriously compromised, not only for the animal and plant world, but also for us humans. As early as 1953, Giono used the term 'natural foundations of live', which is now at the forefront of debates about responsibility for present and future generations. In this context, reference should be made, for example, to the wording of Article 20a of the

92 Ibid., p. 8.
93 Ibid.
94 Cf. ibid., p. 30.
95 Ibid., p. 28.
96 Cf. ibid., p. 18.
97 Cf. ibid., pp. 21–22.
98 Ibid., p. 23.
99 Ibid., p. 24.
100 Ibid., pp. 32–33.
101 Knauβ (2020), p. 225.

German Basic Law: "Mindful also of its responsibility toward future generations, the state shall protect the natural foundations of life and animals by legislation and, in accordance with law and justice, by executive and judicial action, all within the framework of the constitutional order." In this sense, Giono's story seems incredibly far-sighted and anticipatory. It presents a biocentric worldview that is being debated today in the context of countless reflections on the possible applications of the *traditional ecological knowledge* (TEK) of indigenous peoples. It seems that, in Giono's understanding, it is not the anthropocentric but rather the biocentric worldview that leads to 'happiness' and the 'good life'.[102] Everybody can contribute to this 'happiness', if one follows the words of the narrator in *The Man Who Planted Trees:* "When you remembered that all this has sprung from the hands and the soul of this one man, without technical resources, you understand that men could be as effectual as God in other realms than that of destruction".[103] This statement is intended to encourage everyone to act and sounds like a confident commitment to individual agency, provided it is accompanied by will and perseverance.

3.3 Human Beings' Responsibility as Trustees and Guardians

Article 25 of the 2007 *United Nations Declaration on the Rights of Indigenous Peoples* echoes the recognition and trust that indigenous peoples know how to preserve and manage nature, the basis of life for all of us: "Indigenous peoples have the right to maintain and strengthen their distinctive spiritual relationship with their traditionally owned or otherwise occupied and used lands, territories, waters and coastal seas and other resources [...]." In line with Hans Jonas's principle of stewardship, responsibility for preserving our natural resources is collective and applies to both the present and the future. It does not exclude individual responsibility but rather expands it to include an altruistic-collective and preventive component. In *The Man Who Planted Trees,* both forms of responsibility come to bear in the character of Elzéard Bouffier, as his decisions and actions are guided not by individual egocentric considerations, but by biocentric collective ones. This is already evident in his decision to take the initiative to plant trees in response to the desertification and drying up of the region due to a lack of forestation.[104] Elzéard's spontaneous action for the collective good reveals an understanding of the non-human as common property in the sense of the indigenous *Pachamama*, in that he plants trees incessantly, over many kilometres, without asking who owns the land.[105] For him, it goes without saying that it belongs to him, to everyone else and to everything else. Nature and humans are, in a sense, connected to each other through the common

[102] Cf. Giono (1999), p. 28.

[103] Ibid., p. 23.

[104] Cf. ibid., p. 16.

[105] Cf. ibid., pp. 15–16.

ground. Elzéard feels responsible for this ground on behalf of a collective and spontaneously takes on the role of caring for and protecting it. When he realises that his sheep are damaging the young trees, he switches to beekeeping.[106] This gesture once again reflects his biocentric attitude towards the legal entity of soil and earth: nature is more important to him than his professional activity if it proves harmful to it. As a responsible trustee of nature and the trees he plants, nurtures and protects, Elzéard fulfils a precautionary function for future generations, which is increasingly being discussed today. Jean-Philippe Pierron also refers to this when he writes: "Planting means caring about a future that does not concern us, with the tree representing the link between individual, social and cosmological time. This explains why trees and forests are becoming preferred symbols for to make the concept of sustainability tangible".[107]

Since the public forestry authority knows nothing about Elzéard's individual reforestation measures, it assumes, with astonishment, that this must be the first 'naturally' grown forest since the massive deforestation.[108] It is the fact that this is a 'curiosity', rather than any awareness of their responsibility to care for it, that prompts the authorities to place the forest under the protection of three forestry officials and to take strict action against attempts by charcoal burners to bribe them or exploit the forest.[109] Giono's emphasis on the surprise effect of the seemingly 'natural' forest contains an additional criticism of human egoism: "If he had been detected he would have had opposition. He was undetectable. Who in the villages or in the administration could have dreamed of such perseverance in a magnificent generosity?"[110] From this, we can conclude that the forest would not have benefitted from protection if the authorities had learned that their authority had been bypassed. Their personal vanity would have been hurt by the questioning of hierarchy and authority. Giono fundamentally doubts that selfish interests will be set aside in favour of the common good of the 'forest'. In this sense, he anticipates the difficulty we face today in Western society in moving away from its individualistic, anthropocentric paradigms in favour of collective, biocentric ways of thinking and acting. However, this does not mean that we have lost faith in the ability of Cartesian-minded people to change and adopt biocentric values. Cultural and intellectual structures do not prohibit this; rather, egoism and weakness of will are the most powerful obstacles on the path to a cultural, moral and legal change in worldview.

---

[106] Cf. ibid., p. 21.

[107] Pierron (2012), p. 19.

[108] Cf. Giono (1999), p. 25.

[109] Cf. ibid., p. 26.

[110] Ibid., p. 24.

4 Conclusion

Despite its brevity, Giono's story *The Man Who Planted Trees* is an example of poetic power beyond fiction: its publication was followed by actual reforestation campaigns and concrete reforestation measures.[111] By presenting the individual fate of Elzéard Bouffier, it creates a concrete relationship between the reader and the eco-socio-political issues dealt with in the narrative. By embedding his story in an equally concrete, geographically narrowly defined territory, Giono's proposals for action to improve the environment appear tangible and comprehensible. For, as Bachelard aptly puts it, humans lose their ability to act in the vague immensity of the space that is 'the world': "The formulas 'being-in-the-world' and 'the essence of the world' are too 'majestic' for me, I cannot grasp them. I feel more comfortable in a miniature world. When I live in it, I feel waves of world-changing energy emanating from my dreaming being".[112]

Erich Maria Remarque recognised the 'recipe' for an impressive literary message back in 1948, albeit in the context of the Second World War, which had just ended. Nevertheless, the approach and the expected reception remain the same:

> The difficulty lies in the fact that we cannot rely on our imagination. When I say five million died, this number means nothing. Five million deaths are not the same as one death [...]. But if I say five died, then this difficulty could be overcome. And if I tell you that one died – a person I created for you so that you would know and understand him [...], then perhaps I have told you something you should know about the Nazis.[113]

Giono's endeavour to illustrate the close interconnection between culture and nature, between people and their environment, runs through many of his works. As early as 1932, in *The Solitude of Compassion* (1934), Giono alludes to the now much invoked biocentric vision of harmonious coexistence between the human and the non-human as equal legal subjects when he calls for humans to treat nature with modesty and respect:

> I am well aware that a novel without people is hardly conceivable. But they must be set back in their place. They must not constantly be the centre of attention. One must be modest enough to perceive not only the height and width of a mountain, but also its weight, its scent, its gestures, its magic, its words and its sympathies.[114]

In *Lettres aux paysans,* Giono calls for cooperation with nature.[115] As early as 1932, he was aware of human arrogance and domineeringness towards nature. More than ninety years before today's debates on the problems of the anthropocentric world view of the Western world, he called for nature to be treated with respect and modesty. In 1953, in his story *The Man Who Planted Trees,* Giono still conveyed hope

[111] Cf. Pierron (2012), p. 14; Trout and Visser (2006), p. 40.

[112] Bachelard (1989), p. 150.

[113] Van Gelder (1948), p. 256.

[114] Giono (1932), p. 536.

[115] Giono (1989), p. 15.

for the possible salvation and improvement of our planet Earth. But in view of human inertia, his optimism seems to have given way to a more sombre mood years later, in 1970:

> We are obviously in a different era. We must take stock. We receive a legacy from nature and our ancestors. Landscapes reflect states of mind and will continue to do so – for us, and for those who follow us. History is engraved in the stones of monuments. The complete erasure of the past inevitably leads to the inhuman desiccation of the future. We are witnesses to rapid processes of change that do not always bring progress. Our 'beautiful' creations can be counted on one hand, while our 'destructions' are countless.[116]

Giono's anticipatory foresight commands respect. Concentrated in the few pages of *The Man Who Planted Trees* is a foreshadowing of our current dilemmas and debates in the context of the rapidly advancing and continuing destruction of the world, which actually calls our survival into question: Cartesian thinking in separate categories, the 'legal subject human being' in relation to the 'legal object nature', the recognition of holistic interactions in Latour's and Lovelock's Gaia, the necessary exchange of the anthropocentric for a biocentric model of life, the concept of sustainability and the foundations of life, responsibility for present and future generations, the concept of stewardship and caring responsibility. That is a lot of foresight in few pages.

Giono proves with his own example that Western industrial cultures can also change their thinking. It is not insurmountable for our legal systems to understand humans "as part of nature and the world as an entirely interconnected whole in which no part has the right to dominate another part".[117] If Alexander von Humboldt, Jean Giono, Bruno Latour, Gaston Bachelard, Michel Serres, Arne Næss, Klaus Bosselmann, Tilo Wesche, Arturo Escobar, Philippe Descola, Catherine Larrère, Marie-Angèle Hermitte, Olivier Barrière, Alexandre Zabalza, Camille de Toledo, Baptiste Morizot, and many others can develop and defend biocentric concepts and perspectives on an individual level, why should this not also work on a collective level?

In *The Man Who Planted Trees,* Giono still trusts in the power of action of everyone. Almost twenty years later, he loses this trust. How about we give it back to him?

International Declarations

UN World Charter for Nature, 28 October 1982. https://ejcj.orfaleacenter.ucsb.edu/wp-content/uploads/2018/03/1982.-UN-World-Charter-for-Nature-1982.pdf (accessed 30 November 2025).

Earth Charter, 2000. https://earthcharter.org/about-the-earth-charter/ (accessed 30 November 2025).

[116] Giono (1988), p. 83.

[117] Rametsteiner (2025), p. 32.

United Nations Declaration on the Rights of Indigenous Peoples (UNDRIP), 2007. https://www.un.org/development/desa/Indigenouspeoples/wp-content/uploads/sites/19/2018/11/UNDRIP_E_web.pdf (accessed on 28 November 2025)

International Legal Texts

Convention on Biological Diversity (CBD), 1993. https://www.cbd.int/doc/legal/cbd-en.pdf (accessed on 28 November 2025).

Ecuador

Constitution of the Republic of Ecuador 2008, published in Registro Oficial 449 on 20 October 2008 https://www.defensa.gob.ec/wp-content/uploads/downloads/2021/02/Constitucion-de-la-Republica-del-Ecuador_act_ene-2021.pdf (accessed on 26 November 2025)

Colombia

Corte Constitucional 10 November 2016, T-622 (Río Atrato);
Supreme Court of Justice 5 April 2018, STC4360-2018 (Amazonia);
Supreme Court of Justice 18 June 2020, STC3872-2020 (Isla Salamanca).

Bolivia

Law No. 8071 on the Rights of Mother Earth. https://www.planificacion.gob.bo/uploads/marco-legal/Ley%20N%C2%B0%20071%20DERECHOS%20DE%20LA%20MADRE%20TIERRA.pdf (accessed on 26 November 2025).

Canada

Supreme Court of Canada, Haida Nation v. British Columbia, 18 November 2004 (2004 SCC 73, case no. 29419).
Supreme Court of Canada, Taku River Tlingit First Nation v. British Columbia, 18 November 2004 (3 SCR 550, case no. 29146).

New Zealand

Te Urewera Act, 27 July 2014. www.legislation.govt.nz/act/public/2014/0051/latest/whole.html (accessed on 26 November 2025).

Te Awa Tupua (Whanganui River Claims Settlement) Act 2017, 20 March 2017.www.legislation.govt.nz/act/public/2017/0007/latest/whole.html (accessed on 26 November 2025).

Spain

Mar Menor Act, Law 19/2022, of 30 September. https://www.boe.es/eli/es/l/2022/09/30/19 (accessed on 26 November 2025).

References

Auerochs, Florian. 2022. Unverrottbar. Zur Ökologisierung der Ruine im 'toxischen Anthropozän'. In *Anthropozäne Literatur. Poetiken – Genres – Lektüren (Anthropocene Literature. Poetics – Genres – Readings)*, ed. Gabriele Dürbeck et al., vol. 1. Berlin: Springer.

Bachelard, Gaston. 1983. *La poétique de l'espace*. Paris: PUF.

Barrière, Olivier. 2022. La solidarité écologique, lien de droit d'une interdépendance au vivant. In *VertigO*, special edition 37.

Barrière, Olivier, et al., eds. 2019. *Coviability of Social and Ecological Systems: Reconnecting Mankind to the Biosphere in an Era of Global Change (2 vols.)*. Cham: Springer.

Bate, Jonathan. 1991. *Romantic Ecology. Wordsworth and the Environmental Tradition*. London: Routledge.

Berry, Thomas. 2006. *Evening Thoughts: Reflecting on Earth as a Sacred Community*. Berkeley: Counterpoint.

Blanc, Nathalie, et al. 2008. Littérature & écologie: vers une écopoétique. *Écologie & Politique* 36 (2):

Bosselmann, Klaus. 2024. The Framework of Ecological Law. *Environmental Policy and Law* 50:479–486.

Buell, Lawrence. 1991. *The Environmental Imagination. Thoreau, Nature Writing and the Formation of American Culture*. Massachusetts/London: Harvard University Press.

Camproux Duffrène, Marie-Pierre. 2022. Les communs naturels comme expression de la solidarité écologique. In *VertigO*, special edition 37.

Choné, Aurélie. 2019. *Ecocriticism/écocritique* im deutschen und französischen Kontext: eine vergleichende Perspektive. *Revue d'Allemagne et des pays de langue allemande* 51 (2): 321–341.

Citron, Pierre. 1995. *Giono*. Paris: Seuil.

Corsani, Gabriele. 2015. La ricetta di Jean Giono. Rammendi di paesaggi rurali. *RI.VISTA Research for Landscape Architecture* 13 (2): 8–17.

de Toledo, Camille. 2021. *Le fleuve qui voulait écrire: Les auditions du parlement de Loire*, Narrated by Camille de Toledo. Paris: Manuella Éditions.

Delzangles, Hubert, and Alexandre Zabalza. 2023. La reconnaissance, en Espagne, de la personnalité juridique et de droits accordés à la Mar Menor. *AFDA*606–616.

Descartes, René. 2011 [1637]. *Discours de la méthode*. Hamburg: Meiner.

Descola, Philippe. 2005. *Par-delà nature et culture*. Paris: Gallimard.

Escobar, Arturo. 2018. *Sentir-Penser avec la terre, une écologie au-delà de l'occident*. Paris: Seuil-Anthropocène.

Fischer, Ludwig. 2019. *Natur im Sinn. Naturwahrnehmung und Literatur*. Berlin: Matthes & Seitz.

Focus Agate. 2024. The Great Men of the Mountain Land Restoration: Prosper Demontzy, Pascale Hénaut. In INRAE-DipSO, January 2024. https://agate.inrae.fr/agate/en/content/great-men-mountain-land-restoration-prosper-demontzey?utm_source=chatgpt.com (accessed on 1 December 2025).

France Nature Environnement. 2025. "Les Alpes du Sud au défi de la transition écologique", 20 February 2025. https://fnepaca.fr/dossiers/les-alpes-du-sud-au-defi-de-la-transition-ecologique (accessed on 1 December 2025).

Van Gelder, Robert. 1948. *Prominente plaudern*. Vienna: Humboldt.

Giono, Jean. 1932. *Solitude de la Pitié*. Œuvres Romanesques Complètes, vol. I. Paris: Gallimard (éditions Pléiade).

Giono, Jean. 1988. *La Chasse au bonheur*. Paris: Gallimard.

Giono, Jean. 1989. *Lettre aux paysans*. Paris: Gallimard (Récits et Essais, éditions Pléiade).

Giono, Jean. 1999. *The Man Who Planted Trees*, ed. by the Indian Friends of Elzéard Bouffier. https://www.arvindguptatoys.com/arvindgupta/manplantedtrees.pdf (accessed on 19 December 2025).

Glotfelty, Cheryll, and Harold Fromm. 1996. *The Ecocriticism Reader: Landmarks in Literary Ecology*. Athens: University of Georgia Press.

Goldstein, Jürgen. 2018. Nature Writing. Die Natur in den Erscheinungsräumen der Sprache. *Dritte Natur* 1:100–113.

Goldstein, Jürgen. 2019. *Naturerscheinungen. Die Sprachlandschaften des Nature Writing*. Berlin: Matthes & Seitz.

Gomez-Muller, Alfred. 2024. *Les droits de la Terre-Mère. Nature, Pachamama et buen vivir*. Wildproject.

Goodbody, Axel. 2007a. Introduction. In *Nature, Technology and Cultural Change in Twentieth-Century German Literature. The Challenge of Ecocriticism*, ed. Axel Goodbody, viii–xiv. New York: Palgrave Macmillan.

Goodbody, Axel. 2007b. Nature in German Culture: The Role of Writers in Environmental Debate. In *Nature, Technology and Cultural Change in Twentieth-Century German Literature. The Challenge of Ecocriticism*, ed. Axel Goodbody, 3–44. New York: Palgrave Macmillan.

Hermitte, Marie-Angèle. 1988. Le concept de diversité biologique et la création d'un statut de la nature. In *L'Homme, la nature et le droit*, ed. Bernard Edelman and Marie-Angèle Hermitte, 238–372. Paris: Christian Bourgeois.

Hermitte, Marie-Angèle. 2011. La nature, sujet de droit ? *Annales. Histoire, Sciences Sociales*173–212.

Hermitte, Marie-Angèle. 2023. Quelle type de personnalité juridique pour les entités naturelles. In *Droits des êtres humains et droits des autres entités: une nouvelle frontière?* ed. Jean-Pierre Marguénaud and Claire Vial, 83–127. Kremlin-Bicêtre: mare & martin.

Hoppmann, Vincent. 2025. Comparative Law and the Global South Gap: An Empirical Analysis of Comparative Legal Academia in Germany. *Zeitschrift für Vergleichende Rechtswissenschaft (ZvglRWiss)* 124:441–469.

Kanz, Christine. 2023. Kritisches Naturschreiben im Horizont des Anthropozäns: Marion Poschmann, Esther Kinsky, Judith Schalansky und Ulrike Draesner. In *Welche Natur? Und welche Literatur? Traditionen, Wandlungen und Perspektiven des Nature Writing*, ed. Tanja van Hoorn and Ludwig Fischer, 27–46. Berlin: J. B. Metzler.

Knauβ, Stefan. 2020. Pachamama als Ökosystemintegrität – Die Rechte der Natur in der Verfassung von Ecuador und ihre umweltethische Rechtfertigung. *Zeitschrift für praktische Philosophie* 7 (2): 221–244.

Kurt, Hildegard, and Andreas Weber. 2015. *Lebendigkeit sei! Für eine Politik des Lebens. Ein Manifest für das Anthropozän*. Klein Jasedow: ThinkOya.

Latour, Bruno. 2020. *Kampf um Gaia. Acht Vorträge über das neue Klimaregime*. Berlin: Suhrkamp.

Lenk, Hans. 2021. Das Prinzip Verantwortung: Systemverantwortung. In *Hans Jonas Handbuch. Leben – Werk – Wirkung*, ed. Michael Bongardt et al. Berlin: J. B. Metzler.

Leopold, Aldo. 1971. *A Sand County Almanac with Essays on Conservation from Round River*. San Francisco/New York: Ballantine Books.

Leroux, Gilles. 2024. Restaurer la montagne: le temps des forestiers de 1827 à nos jours. In *Les Clionautes*, 11 October 2024. https://www.clionautes.org/restaurer-la-montagne-le-temps-des-forestiers-de-1827-a-nos-jours.html (accessed 1 December 2025).

Liendo Tagle, Illa. 2025. Una victoria Ambiental para las guardianas del lago Titicaca. In *El País*, 13.11.2025.

Marion, Annabelle. 2020. Le Retour d'un auteur: Jean Giono dans l'immédiate après-guerre. *French Studies Bulletin* 41 (154): 30–33.

Michelot, Agnès. 2022. Introduction: Ecological Solidarity: What Prospects for a New Principle of Environmental Law? *VertigO*, special issue 37.

Morizot, Baptiste, and Suzanne Husky. 2024. *Rendre l'eau à la terre: Alliance dans les rivières face au chaos climatique*. Arles: Actes Sud.

Morris, Claire. 1964. The Rights and Duties of Beasts and Trees: A Law Teacher's Essay for Landscape Architects. *Journal of Legal Education* 17 (2): 185–192.

Mortensen, Peter. 2017. 'A Project to Establish Joy': Jean Giono, Happiness and the Framing of Environmentalism. *Green Letters: Studies in Econcriticism* 21 (2): 185–198.

Næss, Arne. 1972. *Shallow and the Deep*. Oslo: Inquiry.

Nelson, Melissa K., and Dan Shilling, eds. 2018. *Traditional Ecological Knowledge: Learning from Indigenous Practices for Environmental Sustainability (New Directions in Sustainability and Society)*. Cambridge: Cambridge University Press.

Nicolas-Le Strat, Pascal. 2018. *Quand la sociologie entre dans l'action – la recherche en situation d'expérimentation sociale, artistique ou politique*. Rennes: Éditions du Commun.

Orsenna, Erik. 2025. *Adopte ta rivière*. Paris: L'Iconoclaste.

Pardé, Jean. 1998. Il y a cent ans: Prosper Demontzey (1831-1898) et l'essor de la RTM. *Revue forestière française* 50 (3): 277–282.

Pelizzon, Alessandro. 2025. *Ecological Jurisprudence. The Law of Nature and the Nature of Law*. Cham: Springer.

Pierron, Jean-Philippe. 2012. Poétique de l'arbre et de la forêt: une lecture bachelardienne de l'œuvre de Jean Giono. In *Altre Modernità*, October 2012, 11–23. https://doi.org/10.13130/2035-7680/2400 (accessed on 2 December 2025).

Rametsteiner, Tina. 2025. *Rechte der Natur. Eine rechtsvergleichende Untersuchung unter besonderer Berücksichtigung der Rechte von Flüssen*. Berlin: Duncker & Humblot.

Routley, Richard. 1973. Is there a need for a new, an environmental, ethic? In *Proceedings of the XVth World Congress of Philosophy*, vol. 1, 205–210. Varna: Sofia Press.

Serrat, Olivier. 2025. *The Man Who Planted Trees*: Ecotopian Ideals in Giono's (1953) Storytelling. In *Olivier Serrat: Anthropogenic Solutions for Climate Change*, 99–102. Singapore: Springer.

Serres, Michel. 2018. *Le contrat naturel*. Paris: PUF.

Simmel, Georg. 1919. Die Ruine. In *Collected Essays, Georg Simmel (Philosophische Kultur)*, 125–133. Leipzig: Kröner.

Soentgen, Jens. 1997. *Das Unscheinbare. Phänomenologische Beschreibungen von Stoffen, Dingen und fraktalen Gebilden*. Berlin: Akademie.

Stone, Christopher D. 1972. Should Trees Have Standing - Towards Legal Rights for Natural Objects. *Southern California Law Review* 45 (1972): 450–501.

Trout, Colette, and Derk Visser. 2006. *Jean Giono*. Amsterdam: Rodopi.

Tsing, Anna Lowenhaupt. 2019. *Der Pilz am Ende der Welt. Über das Leben in den Ruinen des Kapitalismus*. Berlin: Matthes & Seitz.

von Humboldt, Alexander. 1849. *Ansichten der Natur. Mit wissenschaftlichen Erläuterungen*, 2 volumes. Stuttgart: Cotta'scher Verlag.

von Humboldt, Alexander. 2003. In *Reise auf dem Río Magdalena, durch die Anden und Mexico, Part 2*, ed. Margot Faak. Berlin: Akademie Verlag.

Wesche, Tilo. 2023. *Die Rechte der Natur*. Berlin: Suhrkamp.
Weydt, Elisabeth. 2023. *Die Natur hat Recht. Wenn Tiere, Wälder und Flüsse vor Gericht ziehen – für ein radikales Umdenken im Miteinander von Mensch und Natur*. Munich: Knesebeck.
Wulf, Andrea. 2016. *Alexander von Humboldt und die Erfindung der Natur*. Munich: Penguin.
Zapf, Hubert. 2002. *Literatur als kulturelle Ökologie: Zur kulturellen Funktion imaginativer Texte an Beispielen des amerikanischen Romans*. Tübingen: Niemeyer.
Zapf, Hubert. 2008. Literary Ecology and the Ethics of Texts. *New Literary History* 39 (4): 847–868.

From Beaver Alliances to River Parliaments: New Legal Narratives and Interspecies Representation in Contemporary French Literature

Justine Scarlaken

Abstract This chapter examines how contemporary French literature actively participates in the production of Rights of Nature through collaborative devices and hybrid forms. Analysing Camille de Toledo's *Le fleuve qui voulait écrire* (2021) and Baptiste Morizot and Suzanne Husky's *Rendre l'eau à la terre* (2024), it demonstrates that these works represent legal transformation but perform the epistemological, affective, and normative conditions necessary for recognizing non-human entities as legal subjects. Building on Christopher Stone's foundational 1972 theory of legal performativity, the chapter shows how Toledo fictionalizes institutions (the Parliament of Loire), while Morizot and Husky visualize ecological knowledge through watercolours and deep time narratives. These literary strategies create what Stone called a necessary myth that fits contemporary scientific knowledge, offering biosemiotics-based legal animism that legitimizes the redistribution of territorial authority to non-human actors. The chapter thus defends literature as an instituting form of thought that provides law with the cultural and affective foundations it cannot generate alone.

Keywords Rights of Nature · Legal fiction · Performativity · Biosemiotics · Interspecies · Democracy

The Capitalocene confronts modern law with a fundamental aporia: how can legal systems designed to protect private property and facilitate capital accumulation address ecological crises that transcend national boundaries, human temporalities, and the subject-object divide? As Camille de Toledo observes in *Le fleuve qui voulait écrire* (2021), states and capitalism are "le fruit de la loi, d'une certaine écriture de la loi"—the product of law, of a certain way of writing law. The legal fictions that animated nineteenth-century corporate personhood now threaten planetary habitability. Yet law's notorious conservatism—its reliance on precedent, its horror vacui,

J. Scarlaken (✉)
University of Oviedo, Oviedo, Spain
e-mail: scarlakenjustine@uniovi.es

A. Juster (ed.), *Legal Drafts in Anthropocene Literature*, SpringerBriefs in Law,
https://doi.org/10.1007/978-3-032-27283-6_4

its tautological self-reference—makes it structurally resistant to the radical ontological transformation required by the Capitalocene's unprecedented situation.

Against this backdrop, what Toledo calls a "soulèvement légal terrestre"—a terrestrial legal uprising—has emerged to grant legal personhood to natural entities.[1] Ecuador's 2008 Constitution recognized the rights of Pachamama; New Zealand's 2017 *Te Awa Tupua Act* granted the Whanganui River legal standing as "an indivisible and living whole"; Colombia's Constitutional Court acknowledged the rights of the Atrato River and future generations in 2016. These juridical innovations share a common challenge identified by American legal scholar Christopher Stone in his foundational 1972 essay *Should Trees Have Standing?*: how can a guardian know a river's needs? How can non-human entities participate in legal and political decision-making when they cannot speak in human language? Stone's response—that natural objects "can communicate their wants (needs) to us, and in ways that are not terribly ambiguous"[2]—remained largely theoretical, offering three operational criteria (standing, injury recognition, beneficiary status) but little guidance on the practical epistemology of representation.

Contemporary French literature has taken up Stone's unresolved challenge through distinctive formal and collaborative strategies. Toledo's *Le fleuve qui voulait écrire* documents a multi-year parliamentary commission investigating the legal personhood of the Loire River, staging public hearings where jurists, scientists, artists, and riverside inhabitants testify about the river's needs. Rather than proposing legal reform, Toledo's Parliament of Loire enacts what he calls a "fiction institutionnelle territorial"—territorial institutional fiction—that performs the deliberative processes through which humans might learn to recognize nature's authority.[3] Similarly, Baptiste Morizot and Suzanne Husky's *Rendre l'eau à la terre: Alliance dans les rivières face au chaos climatique* (2024) visualizes interspecies collaboration through watercolours painted with river water itself, materializing what they term "*alterintelligence*"—the eight-million-year hydraulic expertise of the beaver—as a legitimate basis for redistributing territorial governance.[4]

These works exemplify a shift in environmental literature from representation to institution-building. Where earlier ecocritical writing documented ecological destruction or imagined post-apocalyptic futures, Toledo and Morizot/Husky actively participate in fabricating the juridical categories and cultural frameworks that Rights of Nature requires. Toledo's hearings produce a normative declaration specifying the Loire's rights to exist, regenerate, and assert its interests. Morizot and Husky develop what they call "médecine castor"—beaver medicine—a restoration philosophy that delegates decision-making authority to non-human ecosystem engineers whose evolutionary expertise exceeds human knowledge.[5] Literature

[1] de Toledo (2021), p. 13.

[2] Stone (1972), p. 11.

[3] de Toledo (2021), p. 286.

[4] Morizot and Husky (2024), p. 14.

[5] Ibid., p. 119.

functions not as commentary on law but as a laboratory for juridical innovation, creating what Stone called the new myth necessary to legitimize recognizing nature as legal subject.

This chapter demonstrates that contemporary French literature functions as an instituting form of thought indispensable to juridical transformation in the Capitalocene. Following Stone's insight that legal vocabulary itself steers judicial interpretation, I analyze how these works create performative language ("verbes d'action",[6] "souverain entrelacé",[7] "médecine castor"[8]) that translates non-human interests into cognizable legal claims. I examine how they resolve Stone's guardian problem through sophisticated epistemologies grounded in biosemiotics, scientific instrumentation, and artistic mediation. And I show how they generate the contemporary myth Stone called for—one that integrates ecological science with political reimagination to produce what Marie-Angèle Hermitte terms "animisme juridique":[9] a rational, science-based framework for re-animating what modernity has de-animated.[10]

This analysis intervenes in three scholarly conversations. Within law and literature studies, it demonstrates literature's capacity not merely to critique law but to actively participate in its fabrication, functioning as what Toledo calls a "service public de l'imaginaire"—a public service of the imaginary that creates the cultural conditions for juridical innovation.[11] Within environmental humanities, it shows how French ecocritical writing engages with global Rights of Nature movements while foregrounding distinctively French theoretical traditions (Latourian actor-network theory, biosemiotics, institutional critique, Latour, Bruno. 1987). Within the growing field of multispecies studies, it examines how literature operationalizes concepts like interspecies democracy and more-than-human representation through concrete apparatus—hearings, watercolours, declarations—rather than remaining at the level of theory.

Methodologically, this chapter analyses literature as a form of legal thought and juridical production, attending to formal choices (genre, narrative structure, visual elements) as tools that shape legal imagination. I am not a legal scholar evaluating the technical validity of these proposals, but a literary scholar examining how literary forms participate in producing juridical categories. My approach treats the auditions, watercolours, and declarations not as illustrations of legal concepts but as literary devices that perform epistemological and affective labour: they translate non-human communication, they visualize lost ecological memory, they stage the

---

[6] Unless otherwise indicated, all translations from French are my own: action verbs.

[7] Entangled sovereign.

[8] Beaver medicine.

[9] Legal animism.

[10] de Toledo (2021), p. 303.

[11] Ibid., p. 19.

deliberative processes through which humans might learn to "penser comme un castor".[12]

The chapter proceeds through Stone's 1972 foundational theory, Toledo's Parliament of Loire as institutional fiction, Morizot and Husky's Beaver Alliance as epistemological hybrid, and concludes by theorizing literature's distinctive capacities and necessary limits in producing juridical transformation.

1 Stone and the Performative Dimension of Legal Language (1972)

1.1 The Contemporary River Moment

We are living through what might be called a river moment: a convergence of ecological urgency, juridical innovations, and epistemological transformations that place aquatic ecosystems at the heart of political and cultural reconfigurations. This moment unfolds within a context of systemic crisis: successive IPCC reports since 2018 have established an implacable diagnosis of climate warming, while the Living Planet Report documents an 85% collapse of freshwater species since 1970.[13] Simultaneously, legal recognition of rivers is multiplying across the globe: following the pioneering cases of Ecuador, New Zealand, and Colombia, India recognized the Ganges and Yamuna as living entities in 2017; Bangladesh granted legal personhood to all its rivers in 2019; Quebec has been debating since 2021 whether to grant rights to the Magpie River.

This section situates these juridical developments within the broader ecological and epistemological context that makes them intelligible. Two convergent phenomena—one juridical and scientific, the other cultural and conceptual—frame the literary interventions analysed in the following sections. The first is the proliferation of legal recognition for rivers; the second is the rehabilitation of the beaver as a figure of non-human ecological intelligence, grounded in what biosemiotics—the study of sign processes and communication across all living organisms—has revealed about non-human capacities for meaningful interaction with their environments.

This juridical wave is accompanied by a scientific and epistemological revolution around what we might call the beaver moment. The Eurasian beaver (*Castor fiber*), hunted to near extinction in Europe, has experienced since the 1990s a spectacular return both in ecosystems and in the collective imaginary. A medieval anecdote reveals the depth of our ontological misunderstandings with this creature: in the Middle Ages, monks classified the beaver as fish, allowing its consumption during Lent due to its scaly tail and semi-aquatic life.[14] This erroneous categorization,

[12] Morizot and Husky (2024), p. 119. To think like a beaver.

[13] Cf. WWF (2020).

[14] Cf. Goldman (2013).

mixing taxonomic ingenuity with gastronomic pragmatism, paradoxically contributed to its massive persecution.

Today, the beaver undergoes a conceptual metamorphosis: from problem animal, it becomes keystone species and ecosystem engineer. Research in fluvial geomorphology demonstrates that a beaver family can construct a system of dams and channels benefiting hundreds of other species, regulating floods, filtering water, creating habitat mosaics of exceptional richness.[15] The beaver thus embodies an alter-intelligence—a non-human intelligence forged by eight million years of hydrological experience that challenges our anthropocentric paradigms. As philosopher Baptiste Morizot ironises: "C'est l'humour typique de l'évolution de conférer des pouvoirs cosmiques régénératifs à une créature aussi peu spectaculaire qu'un rongeur".[16]

This convergence between river moment and beaver moment is not fortuitous: it reveals a crisis of ecological imagination. Our representations of "healthy" rivers—fast flows, single channels, stabilized banks—correspond to degraded landscapes that we have naturalized through collective amnesia. What Morizot calls "une amnésie transformée en norme"[17] structures our inability to imagine other possible relations with aquatic environments. Faced with this amnesia, contemporary literature and art propose a reanimation of our ecological imaginaries. Simultaneously, this moment inscribes itself within a decolonial and militant dimension. Cree artist Kent Monkman, in his work *Les castors du Roi*,[18] reclaims the beaver as a symbol of Indigenous resistance against the extractivist colonialism that founded Canadian political economy on the fur trade. Contemporary struggles for river rights are largely anchored in Indigenous cosmologies: the Māori principle "*Ko au te awa, ko te awa ko au*"[19] juridically grounds the recognition of the Whanganui; Amazonian communities in Ecuador mobilized the Andean concept of Pachamama to constitutionalize nature's rights. These references constitute political alliances where Indigenous thought offers ontological frameworks that Western law struggles to generate endogenously.

The rise of Rights of Nature also responds to what Toledo identifies as a structural crisis in the relationship between states and markets. Since the 1980s, as Toledo observes, globalization and deregulation have led to an "intrication toujours plus poussée des États et des acteurs privés"—an increasingly deep entanglement of states and private actors that has undermined the protective environmental law model.[20] State agencies, caught in the double bind of protecting nature while promoting economic development, have failed in their guardian function. The Rights of Nature

---

[15] Cf. Wheaton et al. (2019).

[16] Morizot and Husky (2024), p. 79. It is evolution's typical humor to confer cosmic regenerative powers on a creature as unspectacular as a rodent.

[17] Ibid., p. 150. An amnesia turned into a norm.

[18] *The King's Beavers* (2011).

[19] I am the river and the river is me.

[20] De Toledo (2021), p. 11.

movement responds by introducing new legal actors capable of representing long-term interests and counterbalancing industrial and productive actors.

1.2 Literature as Juridical Laboratory

It is within this context that this chapter examines how contemporary French literature addresses Stone's unresolved questions by creating legal narratives: literary works that do not merely represent juridical transformation but actively participate in its realization. I focus on two major works: Camille de Toledo's collaborative project *Le fleuve qui voulait écrire: Auditions du Parlement de Loire*,[21] which documents a multi-year parliamentary commission investigating the legal personhood of the Loire River; and Baptiste Morizot and Suzanne Husky's hybrid work *Rendre l'eau à la terre: Alliance dans les rivières face au chaos climatique*,[22] combining philosophical essay, ecological science, and watercolour art to theorize interspecies collaboration in watershed restoration.

These works share a distinctive approach to Rights of Nature: they mobilize collaborative devices (public hearings, artist-philosopher partnerships) and hybrid literary forms (institutional fiction, illustrated essay) to perform the epistemological, affective, and normative conditions necessary for legal transformation. Where Stone theorized the performativity of legal language—arguing that "simply speaking that way" of rights "brings into the legal system a flexibility and open-endedness that no series of specifically stated legal rules can capture"[23]—Toledo and Morizot/Husky actualize this performativity through concrete literary and artistic practices. Toledo's Parliament of Loire functions as what he calls a "fiction institutionnelle territorial" or "institution potentielle",[24] staging the deliberative process by which the Loire might acquire legal personhood. Morizot and Husky visualize what they term "alter-intelligence"—the eight-million-year hydraulic expertise of the beaver—through watercolours made with river water itself, creating an aesthetic that "rend sensible et activable une pensée désaltérée de l'eau".[25]

---

[21] The River that Wanted to Write: Hearings of the Parliament of Loire, 2021.

[22] Returning Water to the Earth: Alliance in Rivers Facing Climate Chaos, 2024.

[23] Stone (1972), p. 22.

[24] de Toledo (2021), pp. 286 and 328.

[25] Morizot and Husky (2024), p. 14.

1.3 Stone's Foundational Intervention

Christopher Stone's *Should Trees Have Standing?* emerged not from environmental law expertise but from a pedagogical thought experiment. Teaching property law in 1971, Stone improvised a question to recapture his students' wandering attention: "What would a radically different law-driven consciousness look like? One in which Nature had rights." The uproar that greeted this suggestion launched what would become one of the most influential essays in environmental jurisprudence.[26] Stone's motivation was initially defensive: to "restore my credibility" by demonstrating that granting legal rights to nature was "not incoherent".[27] Yet the essay's timing proved fortuitous: the Sierra Club's lawsuit against Walt Disney's development of Mineral King Valley in California had just been dismissed for lack of standing. Stone proposed a simple inversion: why not name Mineral King itself as the plaintiff, with the Sierra Club serving as its guardian? Justice William O. Douglas cited Stone's not-yet-published article in his dissent, declaring that the suit "would therefore be more properly labelled as Mineral King v. Morton".[28]

1.3.1 The Three Operational Legal Criteria

Stone's core theoretical contribution establishes three criteria that distinguish entities possessing "legal rights in their own right" from those merely protected incidentally through human property interests. First, the entity must have standing, the capacity to institute legal proceedings "at its behest" through a guardian or trustee.[29] Stone emphasizes the operational difference between two slave societies: one where a master can sue for reduced chattel value when someone beats his slave, versus another where the slave can institute proceedings himself for his own recovery, with damages measured by his pain and suffering. Neither society leaves the slave wholly unprotected, but in the second the slave is a holder of rights. Similarly, while pollution of a stream might trigger lawsuits by downstream riparian owners in traditional common law, the stream itself has no standing—it cannot challenge the polluter's actions in its own name.

Second, injury recognition requires courts to account for damage to the entity itself, independent of economic consequences for humans. Stone criticizes how courts engage in balancing that weighs only "the economic hardships on the upper riparian (or dependent community) of abating the pollution vis-à-vis the economic hardships of continued pollution on the lower riparian".[30] What does not enter this

26 Cf. Stone (1972), p. XI.

27 Ibid., p. XII.

28 Ibd., p. XIV.

29 Cf. ibid., p. 4.

30 Ibid., p. 5.

calculus is "the damage to the stream, its fish and turtles and 'lower' life".[31] Stone proposes instead that damages be calculated by the costs of "making the stream whole"—reoxygenating water, restocking fish, repairing watersheds.

Third, beneficiary status requires that legal relief "run to the benefit" of the entity itself, not its human owners.[32] To prevent the environment from being "sold out in a negotiation among private litigants," Stone proposes trust funds administered by guardians.[33] These funds, financed by damages awards and criminal fines, would be available to "preserve the natural object as closely as possible to its condition at the time the environment was made a rights-holder".[34]

1.3.2 The Central Thesis: Performativity of Legal Language

Stone's most radical claim concerns not the technical details of standing and damages but the performative power of legal vocabulary itself. He anticipates the objection that his proposal merely restates existing rules: one could simply say that courts "ought to extend standing" and "ought to weigh environmental damage" without introducing the language of nature having rights. Stone responds that speaking of rights does far more than specify rules. "Introducing the notion of something having a 'right' (simply speaking that way)," he argues, "brings into the legal system a flexibility and open-endedness that no series of specifically stated legal rules like R1, R2, R3... Rn can capture".[35]

The mechanism of this performativity operates through what we might call semantic infiltration: legal terms like "right," "infant," and "corporation" carry "meaning—vague but forceful—in ordinary language, and the force of these meanings, inevitably infused with our thought, becomes part of the context against which the 'legal language' of our contemporary 'legal rules' is interpreted".[36] Stone offers burden of proof as an example: in cases governed by vague rules, "it is context—senses of direction, of value and purpose—that determines how the rules will be understood".[37] Judges who could "unabashedly refer to the 'legal rights of the environment' would be encouraged to develop a viable body of law—in part simply through the availability and force of the expression".[38]

Stone's conclusion merits full quotation: "A society in which it is stated, however vaguely, that 'rivers have legal rights' would evolve a different legal system than one which did not employ that expression, even if the two of them had, at the start,

[31] Ibid., p. 6.

[32] Ibid., p. 4.

[33] Ibid., p. 16.

[34] Ibid., p. 17.

[35] Ibid., p. 22.

[36] Ibid.

[37] Ibid.

[38] Ibid., p. 23.

the very same 'legal rules' in other respects".[39] This claim goes beyond conventional legal realism to assert that vocabulary itself—not merely the interests and ideologies of legal actors—structures the evolution of legal systems.

1.3.3 The Guardian Problem and Stone's Partial Response

Stone confronts the objection that guardians cannot know the needs of rivers or forests: "the very concept of 'needs,' it might be said, could be used here only in the most metaphorical way".[40] His response reveals both the strength and the limits of his 1972 framework. On one hand, he effectively inverts the objection: "I am sure I can judge with more certainty and meaningfulness whether and when my lawn wants (needs) water, than the Attorney General can judge whether and when the United States wants (needs) to take an appeal from an adverse judgment by a lower court".[41] Natural objects communicate their needs through observable signs—"a certain dryness of the blades and soil—immediately obvious to the touch—the appearance of bald spots, yellowing, and a lack of springiness after being walked on".[42] These signals are "not terribly ambiguous" and far less metaphysical than the wants attributed to corporations or nation-states.

On the other hand, Stone provides little guidance on the epistemology of translation beyond this analogy. Who serves as guardian? Stone suggests it should not be existing government agencies like the Department of Interior, given their conflicts of interest. But his alternative—"some group of persons who could be expected to speak for 'it'"—remains vague.[43] The question of how scientific knowledge, local experience, and aesthetic judgment should be weighted in determining an ecosystem's needs goes largely unaddressed.

1.3.4 The Call for a New Cosmic Myth

Stone concludes with what initially appears to be a philosophical digression but proves essential to understanding his project's ambitions. He observes that environmental arguments often rely on utilitarian calculus—protecting wilderness benefits future generations, preserving species guards against unforeseen needs—but finds "something sad about the spectacle" when conservationists argue exclusively this way.[44] Stone advocates instead for "a frank avowal that even making adjustments for

[39] Ibid.

[40] Ibid., p. 11.

[41] Ibid.

[42] Ibid.

[43] Ibid., p. 473.

[44] Ibid., p. 24.

aesthetic improvements, what I am proposing is going to cost 'us,' i.e., reduce our standard of living as measured in terms of our present values".[45]

This economic honesty leads to Stone's most ambitious claim: "The time may be on hand when these sentiments, and the early stirrings of the law, can be coalesced into a radical new theory or myth—felt as well as intellectualized—of man's relationships to the rest of nature".[46] He means myth not pejoratively but as societies have relied on myths "that we are cosigners of a social contract, that the pope is God's agent, and that all men are created equal".[47] Existing nature-centered myths—"Pantheism, Shintoism, and Taoism"—are inadequate because they are "all, each in its own fashion, quaint, primitive, and archaic".[48] What is needed is "a myth that can fit our growing body of knowledge of geophysics, biology and the cosmos".[49]

Stone tentatively suggests viewing Earth "as one organism, of which mankind is a functional part—the mind, perhaps: different from the rest of nature, but different as a man's brain is from his lungs".[50] Yet Stone leaves this mythological project largely undeveloped. His essay concludes with the practical question of standing doctrine, not the philosophical challenge of creating new narratives adequate to Capitalocene knowledge. This incompleteness is not a failure but an invitation—one that contemporary French literature, as we shall see, has accepted.

Stone's 1972 intervention thus establishes three elements crucial for subsequent legal and literary developments: (1) a technical framework specifying what granting rights to nature would operationally require; (2) a theory of legal language's performative power to reshape judicial interpretation and social consciousness; (3) an unfulfilled call for a contemporary myth that integrates scientific knowledge with transformed human-nature relations. The guardian problem—how representatives can know and speak for non-human needs—remains more posed than solved. It is precisely this lacuna that contemporary French literature addresses through its distinctive formal and epistemological strategies.

2 Fictionalizing the Institution—le Parlement de Loire as Juridical Laboratory

If Stone theorized legal language's performative power, Camille de Toledo's *Le fleuve qui voulait écrire* (2021) actualizes that performativity through what its creators call a "fiction institutionnelle territoriale"—a territorial institutional fiction.[51]

[45] Ibid.

[46] Ibid., p. 29.

[47] Ibid.

[48] Ibid.

[49] Ibid.

[50] Ibid.

[51] de Toledo (2021), p. 286.

By this term, Toledo designates a literary work that does not merely describe or imagine a possible institution but enacts its procedures and deliberative practices, thereby producing normative and affective effects in the world despite lacking formal legal authority. The project emerged from a multi-year collaboration involving jurists, philosophers, scientists, artists, and Loire River stakeholders, culminating in public hearings that simulated a parliamentary commission investigating whether the Loire should be granted legal personhood. The resulting book documents these auditions—testimonies by Bruno Latour, Marie-Angèle Hermitte, Frédérique Aït-Touati, Valérie Cabanes, and dozens of others—alongside essays, declarations, and visual materials. Yet to describe the Parliament of Loire merely as documentation misconstrues its fundamental nature: it is not a representation of a potential institution but an enactment of institutional practice, a laboratory where juridical transformation is performed rather than proposed.

2.1 *Institutional Fiction as Actualized Performativity*

Toledo distinguishes his project sharply from utopia: "Nous ne sommes pas les artisans d'un projet utopique. L'utopie, c'est la négation du lieu. *U-topos*".[52] Instead, the Parliament pursues what he terms "récits topiques"—topical narratives: "notre siècle demande des récits non utopiques, mais topiques"—narratives that depart from specific places and return to them.[53] This grounding in the Loire basin's actual ecology, hydrology, and social conflicts distinguishes the project from abstract legal philosophy. The Commission's mandate derives not from existing political authority but from a performative inversion: "La Loire nous mande, la nature nous mande, la Terre nous mande".[54] This reversal transforms nature from passive object of legislation into the sovereign that authorizes human representatives.

The institutional fiction operates through what Toledo calls a "service public de l'imaginaire"—a public service of the imaginary.[55] The phrase is deliberately paradoxical: how can imagination be a public service? Toledo's response hinges on Stone's insight about vocabulary's steering power. Just as nineteenth-century legal fictions (corporate personhood) reshaped economic relations, twenty-first-century legal fictions can reshape ecological relations. The task is to "fictionner autrement"—to fiction differently, to "réécrire les lois"—rewrite the laws by creating imaginative frameworks that law can subsequently formalize.[56] The Parliament thus functions as what Frédérique Aït-Touati calls a "capsule collective, la préparation d'un souverain à venir"—a collective capsule, the preparation of a sovereign to

[52] Ibid., p. 24. We are not the artisans of a utopian project. Utopia is the negation of place. U-topos.

[53] Ibid., p. 14.

[54] Ibid., p. 56. The Loire summons us, nature summons us, the Earth summons us.

[55] Ibid., p. 19.

[56] Ibid., p. 61.

come—an archive for future generations who will legislate under intensified bioclimatic crisis.[57]

This archival dimension is crucial. Bruno Latour, testifying before the Commission, emphasizes that "il n'y a que les fictions pour advancer"—only fictions can move us forward—when confronting the Capitalocene's unprecedented situation.[58] The Parliament of Loire creates what Latour terms "fondations"—foundations—for a legal "château"—castle—that does not yet exist.[59] Without these fictional foundations—the mythologies, vocabularies, and procedural templates that make recognition of natural entities thinkable—the juridical castle remains suspended, impossible to construct. Literature here performs labour that law cannot: it imagines institutional forms before they exist, creating the cultural conditions for their eventual realization.

2.2 *The Auditions: Experimenting with Extended Democracy*

The hearings themselves enact what the project calls "une alterpolitique"—an alterpolitics—that extends democracy beyond the human species.[60] Each audition follows a parliamentary format: the Commission poses questions, the witness responds, commissioners probe for clarification. Yet the substance of testimony systematically challenges anthropocentric assumptions. Marie-Angèle Hermitte explains how "animisme juridique"—legal animism—recognizes that modern law, despite its claims to rationality, has always animated entities: corporations, trusts, foundations.[61] The question is not whether to animate but which entities to animate and how. Hermitte proposes that natural entities require a "droit au traducteur"—right to a translator—analogous to human defendants' right to legal counsel.[62] These translators would form a "constellation" who measure hydraulic stress, render degradation visible, and testify to ecological memory.

Bruno Latour's testimony develops the epistemology of translation. "Les scientifiques sont les meilleurs traducteurs des voix, des langages de la nature"—scientists are the best translators of nature's voices and languages—he argues, because ecological measurement is how nature "n'a jamais cessé de parler"—has never stopped speaking.[63] When hydrologists track sediment flow or bioacousticians record underwater soundscapes, they translate non-human communication into forms cognizable by legal institutions. Yet Latour insists that translation requires

[57] Ibid., p. 22.
[58] Ibid., p. 59.
[59] Ibid., p. 253.
[60] Ibid., p. 78.
[61] Cf. ibid., p. 63.
[62] Cf. ibid., p. 127.
[63] Ibid., p. 85.

more than scientific data: it demands a precise exercise of description to answer the question "Combien d'êtres doivent être pris en compte pour faire Loire ?"—How many beings must be taken into account to make Loire?[64] This descriptive labor reveals the "emmêlement, entrelacs"—entanglement, interlacing—between human and non-human elements.[65]

The hearings also experiment with what the Commission calls "mise en corporalité du sujet"—putting the subject into corporality (de Toledo 2021, p. 132). Hermitte emphasizes that legal efficacy requires "faire entrer leur corps"—making their bodies enter—courtrooms: "l'oiseau mazouté qui impose au tribunal la longue séquence de son agonie"—the oil-covered bird that imposes on the tribunal the long sequence of its agony—proves more persuasive than any expert report (de Toledo 2021, p. 320). The Parliament of Loire thus incorporates practices of "réattachement"—reattachment—walking seasonal ponds, listening to river soundscapes, practicing ecopsychology (de Toledo 2021, p. 427). These embodied practices aim to produce what jurist Laurent Neyret calls a "bascule affective, cognitive"—an affective and cognitive tipping—that must accompany institutional change (de Toledo 2021, p. 286).

2.3 *From Fiction to Norm: The Déclaration des Droits de Loire*

The auditions culminate in the production of normative texts: first a *Manifeste de la Loire*[66] articulating values, then a *Déclaration des droits de Loire*[67] specifying rights and governance structures. This progression from hearing to declaration enacts what Latour's ethnography of the Conseil d'État calls the "ravaudage, un tricotage, un grignotement incessant"—patching, knitting, constant nibbling—by which law evolves.[68] The Declaration emerges from a writing workshop that aggregates scientific knowledge, citizen expertise, situated knowledge, and popular knowledge—gathered during the inquiry.

The Declaration's legal status is deliberately ambiguous. Jurist Laurent Neyret acknowledges that established legal texts would classify it as "de la literature"—literature—rather than "textes normatifs"—normative texts.[69] Yet this literary status proves strategically productive. The Declaration functions as what Anglo-American jurisprudence calls "soft law"—norms that lack immediate enforceability but exert persuasive authority. Its primary audience is not legislators but judges, who might

[64] Ibid., p. 55.

[65] Ibid., p. 59.

[66] Loire Manifesto.

[67] Declaration of Loire's Rights.

[68] Latour (2002), p. 114.

[69] De Toledo (2022), p. 174.

cite it to "faire entrer [le droit] dans le droit"—make law enter into law.[70] Historical precedent exists: Argentina's 2016 recognition of a chimpanzee as rights-holder cited the *Universal Declaration of Animal Rights* to justify an unprecedented ruling. The *Declaration of Loire's Rights* thus operates as what the Commission calls a juridical impulsion, a textual artifact that can create jurisprudence if an audacious judge chooses to mobilize it.

Moreover, the Declaration's literary form allows it to articulate what juridical language cannot. Where law must "découper, séparer juridiquement les éléments"—carve up, legally separate elements—to create justiciable subjects, literature can maintain the "emmêlement"—entanglement—that ecological reality demands.[71] The Declaration specifies the Loire's rights—"droit d'exister", "droit de se régénérer", "droit de faire valoir ses intérêts"—right to exist, right to regenerate, right to assert its interests—while simultaneously insisting on the river's indivisibility.[72]

2.4 *The Myth of the Entangled Sovereign*

The Parliament of Loire's ultimate contribution lies in creating the "new myth" Stone called for. Where Stone's 1972 essay could only sketch the idea of Earth as organism with humanity as "mind," Toledo's project generates a full mythological apparatus adequate to contemporary science. The central figure is what the Commission calls the entangled sovereign a political authority distributed across human and non-human actors rather than concentrated in the modern state's anthropocentric sovereignty.

This myth draws on multiple traditions while remaining resolutely contemporary. Yet it refuses what Toledo calls the temptation to appropriate Indigenous cosmologies as quaint, primitive, archaic solutions. Instead, the entangled sovereign synthesizes Latourian actor-network theory (where agency is always distributed), biosemiotics (where all organisms communicate), and contemporary hydrology (where watersheds constitute indivisible systems). The result is what Hermitte terms science-based legal animism, an ontology that reanimates what modernity de-animated while grounding this reanimation in empirical knowledge of ecological interdependence. The myth's political force lies in its inversion of authority. Traditional sovereignty flows from human collectivities (nations, peoples) that authorize governments to act. The entangled sovereign reverses this flow: "la Loire nous mande" means the river itself becomes the source of mandate.[73] This is a reconception of political legitimacy. When the Commission claims its "seul mandat"—sole mandate—comes from nature, it articulates what Latour calls the shift

---

[70] Ibid., p. 134.

[71] Ibid., p. 193.

[72] Ibid., p. 54.

[73] Ibid., p. 56.

from a "nation anthropocentrée" to a "nation réelle, qui s'ouvrirait aux êtres de la nature"—from anthropocentric nation to real nation that opens itself to nature's beings.[74]

Toledo's Parliament of Loire thus moves Stone's project from theory to practice, from conceptual argument to performed institution. Where Stone theorized performativity, Toledo enacts it. Where Stone posed the guardian problem, Toledo stages the translators' constellation. Where Stone called for a new myth, Toledo generates the myth of the entangled sovereign. Yet crucial questions remain: How do the translators access non-human knowledge? What legitimizes redistributing authority to entities with eight million years of expertise but no human language? It is to these questions that Baptiste Morizot and Suzanne Husky's Beaver Alliance turns, offering both scientific rigor and artistic visualization as responses to Stone's unresolved epistemological challenges.

3 Visualizing and Translating—l'Alliance Castor as Epistemological Hybrid

If Toledo's Parliament of Loire demonstrates how institutional fiction can actualize legal performativity, Baptiste Morizot and Suzanne Husky's *Rendre l'eau à la terre: Alliance dans les rivières face au chaos climatique* (2024) addresses Stone's unresolved epistemological challenge through a distinctive hybrid form: philosophical essay intertwined with watercolour paintings, scientific hydrology integrated with mythological narrative. Where Toledo stages democratic deliberation about granting rivers legal standing, Morizot and Husky demonstrate why such recognition is epistemologically justified and practically urgent.

3.1 Watercolors as Legal Devices

Suzanne Husky's watercolours are not illustrations accompanying Morizot's text but constitute independent epistemological claims. Each painting is created with "une eau qui vient de quelque part"—water that comes from somewhere—a Gironde fountain, a California river—materializing the substance they represent within the artwork itself.[75] This formal choice enacts what the authors call an effort to "rendre sensible et activable une pensée désaltérée de l'eau"—to make a dequenched thinking of water sensible and activatable.[76]

[74] Ibid., p. 259.

[75] Morizot and Husky (2024), p. 13.

[76] Ibid., p. 14.

Joe Wheaton's preface emphasizes the watercolours' scientific precision: they offer "représentations très puissantes – et, d'après mon expérience, précises – des contrastes" between "notre monde asséché"—our desiccated world—and the regenerated world it is possible to imagine.[77] The paintings visualize what Morizot calls "une rivière anabranche"—an anabranching river—a term unfamiliar to most readers, denoting rivers with multiple stable channels separated by vegetated islands, the opposite of the channelized, single-thread rivers that modernity has constructed as the norm.[78]

These images perform crucial labor for Rights of Nature discourse. By visualizing what Morizot calls "lenteurs habitables"—inhabitable slownesses—meandering channels, fallen wood, beaver ponds—the watercolors create "une esthétique de la rivière qui fasse justice à ce qu'elle peut être"—an aesthetic of the river that does justice to what it can be—when functioning fully.[79] A healthy river, the paintings demonstrate, "conjugue un bouquet de verbes": "étangtifier, recharger, inonder, accélérer, ralentir, infuser"—ponds, recharges, floods, accelerates, slows, infuses.[80] These verbs become the vocabulary through which translators can articulate rivers' interests in legal proceedings.

3.2 *Deep Time as Active Power and Beaver Medicine*

Morizot conceptualizes deep time not as "une frise passive"—a passive timeline—but as "une puissance active avec laquelle on peut agir, comme force de régénération"—an active power with which one can act, as a force of regeneration.[81] If the Loire's legal guardians must determine the river's interests, they should consult the only entities with experience managing river health across geological epochs. The beaver becomes what Morizot terms an "ambassadeur"—ambassador—of the "liens intimes et invisibles entre l'eau et la vie"—intimate and invisible links between water and life.[82]

The practical translation of this temporal epistemology is what Morizot terms "la médecine castor"—beaver medicine—"une philosophie de l'"action"[83] for watershed restoration that requires "déléguer et partager la prise de décision avec la rivière et les castors"—delegating and sharing decision-making with the river and beavers.[84] This is not metaphor but operational procedure. Restoration projects

77 Ibid., p. 9.
78 Ibid., p. 55.
79 Ibid., p. 25.
80 Ibid., p. 190.
81 Ibid., p. 160.
82 Ibid., p. 1.
83 A Philosophy of action.
84 Morizot and Husky (2024), p. 119.

employing beaver medicine begin not by imposing human designs but by "accepter que les processus (et non le design humain) dictent la forme initiale du milieu"—accepting that processes (and not human design) dictate the initial form of the environment (Morizot and Husky 2024, p. 119).[85]

This redistribution of authority responds to Stone's concern about democratic legitimacy. Morizot's answer: constrain human decision-making by subordinating it to non-human expertise verified through decades of ecosystem monitoring. The beaver's authority derives not from mystical communion with nature but from measurable capacity to regenerate ecosystem functions.

3.3 Biosemiotics as Translation Foundation

The epistemological foundation enabling this redistribution is what Toledo refers to with biosemiotics—"l'extension de la notion de langage"[86] to recognize that non-human organisms are "de très prolixes et puissants émetteurs et récepteurs et transmetteurs d'informations"—very prolix and powerful emitters and receivers and transmitters of information.[87] The beaver communicates its needs through dam placement, which hydrologists can read as clearly as human engineers read blueprints. The river communicates through sediment grain size, flow velocity, channel morphology—signals that scientific instruments translate into data cognizable by legal institutions.

Having established watercolours as epistemological devices and deep time as an active resource for legal guardianship, Morizot and Husky now address the most fundamental objection to Rights of Nature: how can entities that do not speak human language participate in legal and political processes? Their response mobilizes two interconnected concepts—a conversational model drawn from evolutionary ecology, and the notion of alterintelligence—that together provide the epistemological foundation Stone's 1972 essay lacked. Morizot and Husky resolve the apparent paradox of non-linguistic communication through what they call a "modèle conversationnel"—conversational model: the contingent evolutionary fit between rivers and beavers creates a "relation responsive" where "la rivière et le castor 'répondent' d'une manière telle que la conversation poursuit dans le temps humain"—the river and the beaver 'respond' in such a way that the conversation continues in human time.[88] This conversational model grounds what Morizot calls "alterintelligence"—recognition of non-human intelligence not as inferior approximation of human

---

[85] Ibid.

[86] The expansion of the notion of language.

[87] Morizot and Husky (2024), pp. 16–17.

[88] Ibid., p. 210.

reason but as “un faisceau de relations”—a bundle of relations—evolved over millions of years.[89]

Morizot and Husky’s Beaver Alliance thus provides the epistemological apparatus Stone’s 1972 essay lacked. Where Stone could only assert that natural objects communicate needs “in ways that are not terribly ambiguous,” Morizot and Husky specify the mechanisms: biosemiotic signals, measurable ecosystem metrics, evolutionary expertise verified through adaptive management.

4 Literature’s Power and Limits—Between Critique and Complementarity

Contemporary French literature’s engagement with Rights of Nature demonstrates remarkable lucidity about the political and economic challenges these proposals face. Unlike Stone’s relatively optimistic 1972 essay, Toledo and Morizot/Husky confront the objections that have prevented Rights of Nature from gaining traction in European law while simultaneously theorizing literature’s distinctive capacities and necessary limitations.

4.1 Responding to Critical Objections

The guardian problem that preoccupied Stone receives comprehensive resolution through what Toledo’s collaborators term as a “constellation” of translators. This multi-vocal approach prevents any single constituency from monopolizing representation while grounding guardianship in verifiable ecological knowledge. The economic objections prove more intractable. Stone’s “frank avowal” that granting nature rights would “reduce our standard of living” finds sophisticated development in these works. Rather than retreating to utilitarian justifications, Toledo and Morizot embrace non-utilitarian discourse while acknowledging its political vulnerability. The beaver is valued not for “services écosystémiques”—ecosystem services—but as “puissance continentale” and “aîné”—continental power and elder—with intrinsic worth grounded in eight million years of expertise.[90] Yet conferring legal personhood requires granting patrimoine (assets), which risks what the Loire Commission calls “biocapitalisme”—biocapitalism—transforming rivers into economic actors charging rent for water use.[91] The Commission expresses “pudeur et gêne éthique”—modesty and ethical discomfort—about this prospect, relegating financial questions

[89] Ibid., p. 234.

[90] Ibid., p. 243.

[91] Ibid., p. 334.

to future "scénarios d'anticipation"—anticipation scenarios.[92] This tension—between needing opposable legal status and fearing market recuperation—remains unresolved, a productive aporia these works acknowledge rather than obscure.

The risk of elite appropriation receives direct address through territorial anchoring. Both projects insist on "topique"[93] rather than "utopique"[94] approaches, emphasizing local struggles over abstract principles. The Loire Commission addresses itself to "collectifs humains, hors institutions: territoires, chercheurs, artistes, collectifs citoyens, activists"—human collectives outside institutions.[95] Yet the reliance on civil society raises questions about class composition: who has leisure to attend hearings, commission watercolours, write declarations? The works gesture toward "solidarité ontologique"—ontological solidarity—linking Rights of Nature to historical struggles against objectification, but the concrete mechanisms for ensuring working-class and Global South participation remain underspecified.[96]

4.2 *What Literature Does—and Cannot Do—to Law*

Literature's distinctive capacities operate across three registers. First, it reveals and contests the fiction that govern us. Literary analysis exposes these fictions' contingency and mutability, demonstrating that institutional change requires. Second, literature anchors law in affect and sensibility. Where juridical language abstracts, literary and artistic forms can express "la saveur, le lien aux paysages, la couleur des jours, l'attachement au fleuve"—the savor, the link to landscapes, the color of days, the attachment to the river.[97] This affective dimension is not ornamental but constitutive: the "bascule affective, cognitive"[98] that Neyret identifies as prerequisite for institutional change cannot occur through juridical reasoning alone.[99] Third, literature creates what Latour calls the foundations for legal castles, the ontological frameworks, mythological narratives, and procedural templates that make new legal forms thinkable before they exist.

Yet literature's power is precisely its limitation: it cannot create *opposabilité* (enforceability). As jurists testifying before the Loire Commission emphasize, only law can produce "fiction opposable"—opposable fiction—norms that carry state sanction and can compel action.[100] The *Déclaration des droits de Loire* remains

92 Ibid., p. 333.

93 Place-based.

94 Utopian.

95 de Toledo (2021), p. 489.

96 Ibid., p. 523.

97 Ibid., p. 18.

98 Affective and cognitive shift.

99 de Toledo (2021), p. 286.

100 Ibid., p. 327.

"literature" from the perspective of established legal texts, lacking immediate juridical force. Its power is anticipatory and persuasive: it creates an archive that future judges might cite, but not a rule that courts must apply. Similarly, while Husky's watercolours visualize river health with scientific precision, they cannot by themselves establish legal standards or allocate water rights.

This complementarity suggests that Rights of Nature requires coordinated action across institutional registers. Literature and art create the imaginative and affective conditions—the myths, vocabularies, and sensibilities—that make recognizing natural entities as legal subjects culturally possible. Law translates these cultural shifts into enforceable norms, technical procedures, and institutional structures. Neither suffices alone: literature without law remains utopian archive; law without literature remains abstract technocracy divorced from the affective attachments that motivate political mobilization.

5 Conclusion

From Christopher Stone's 1972 thought experiment to contemporary French literary-juridical laboratories, this chapter has traced how Rights of Nature discourse has evolved from theoretical proposal to performed practice. Stone theorized legal language's performative power but left the guardian problem largely unresolved and his call for a new myth unfulfilled. Contemporary French literature actualizes Stone's insights through distinctive formal and epistemological strategies. Toledo's Parliament of Loire transforms the thought experiment into collective ritual, staging the deliberative processes through which humans might learn to accept nature's mandate. Morizot and Husky's Beaver Alliance visualizes non-human expertise through watercolours made with river water and legitimizes redistributing territorial authority through deep time narratives grounded in evolutionary biology.

These works' signal contribution lies not in solving all objections but in demonstrating that literature functions as an instituting form of thought indispensable to juridical transformation. They create what Stone called for but could not generate: a myth adequate to contemporary scientific knowledge, an epistemology of translation grounded in biosemiotics and artistic mediation, and a political mythology—the entangled sovereign, the beaver elder—that makes interspecies democracy conceptually and affectively possible. Yet they remain lucid about limitations: the risk of market recuperation, the challenge of non-utilitarian discourse in capitalist democracies, the tension between legal separation and ecological entanglement.

While this chapter has focused on the French literary and theoretical context, the strategies it identifies—institutional fiction, hybrid visual-philosophical forms, biosemiotic epistemologies of translation—speak to challenges faced by Rights of Nature movements globally. The Whanganui River's legal personhood in New Zealand, the Atrato River's recognition in Colombia, and the ongoing debates around the Ganges in India all confront the same guardian problem Stone articulated in 1972: how to translate non-human needs into legal language. The French works analysed here offer transferable formal and epistemological resources for this task, particularly their insistence that legal transformation requires not only technical juridical innovation but also the cultural, affective, and imaginative labour that literature distinctively provides. Yet their specificity matters: Toledo's institutional fiction draws on distinctively French traditions of institutional critique and Latourian actor-network theory, while Morizot and Husky's work emerges from a particular philosophical engagement with biosemiotics and field ecology. Future comparative research might examine how literary traditions in other legal and cultural contexts—from Māori storytelling practices that informed New Zealand's *Te Awa Tupua Act* to Latin American testimonial literature accompanying Amazonian environmental struggles—develop analogous but formally distinct strategies for making interspecies representation thinkable and practicable.

As climate crisis intensifies, the question is not whether law will recognize nature's rights but whether this recognition will occur through proactive transformation or catastrophic collapse. Literature, these works demonstrate, provides law with the imaginative resources it cannot generate alone—the foundations for castles not yet built but desperately needed. The Capitalocene demands not merely new statutes but new modes of legal imagination, and contemporary French literature has answered this demand by becoming, in Toledo's phrase, a "service public de l'imaginaire" that makes future law possible.

References

Goldman, Jason. 2013. "Once upon a time, the Catholic Church decided that beavers were fish", BBC Earth, 2013, https://www.scientificamerican.com/blog/thoughtful-animal/once-upon-a-time-thecatholicchurch-decided-that-beavers-were-fish/ (accessed on 13 January 2026).

Hermitte, Marie-Angèle. 2020. Each Object Has Its Own Subject! The Legal Revolutions of the Human Nature Relationship. In *Legal Actions for Future Generations*, ed. Émilie Gaillard and David Forman, 247–270. Bruxelles: Peter Lang.

IPCC. 2023a. In *Climate Change 2022 – Impacts, Adaptation and Vulnerability: Working Group II Contribution to the Sixth Assessment Report of the Intergovernmental Panel on Climate Change*, ed. H.-O. Pörtner et al., 1st ed. Cambridge/New York: Cambridge University Press.

IPCC. 2023b. In *Climate Change 2022 – Mitigation of Climate Change: Working Group III Contribution to the Sixth Assessment Report of the Intergovernmental Panel on Climate Change*, ed. R. Shukla et al. Cambridge/New York: Cambridge University Press.

Latour, Bruno. 1987. *La Science en action. Introduction à la sociologie des sciences*. Paris: La Découverte.

Morizot, Baptiste, and Suzanne Husky. 2024. *Rendre l'eau à la terre: Alliance dans les rivières face au Chaos climatique*. Arles: Actes Sud.

Stone, Christopher. 1972. *Should Trees Have Standing? Law, Morality, and the Environment*. Oxford: Oxford University Press.

Toledo, Camille de. 2021. Le fleuve qui voulait écrire: Les auditions du parlement de Loire. Mise en récit par Camille de Toledo. Paris: Manuella Éditions.

Wheaton, Joe, et al., eds. 2019. Upscaling Site-Scale Ecohydraulic Model to Inform Salmonid Population-Level Life Cycle Modelling and Restoration Actions: Lessons from the Columbia River Basin. *Earth Surface Processes and Landforms* 44 (1): 21–44.

WWF (World Wildlife Fund). 2020. *Living Planet Report 2020: Bending the Curve of Biodiversity Loss*. Gland: WWF International.

“I Am the Cold/I Am the Melt”: Poetic Testimony and the Right to Be Cold in Jessie Kleemann’s *Arkhticós Dolorôs*

Matthew H. Birkhold

Abstract Jessie Kleemann’s *Arkhticós Dolorôs* (2019) offers a searing poetic meditation on Arctic loss from a Kalaallit (Greenlandic Inuit) perspective, transforming grief into a form of legal expression outside the bounds of formal jurisprudence. This contribution explores how Kleemann’s hybrid work—merging poetry, performance, and visual art—functions as an embodied legal draft that interrogates the violence of climate change, colonial erasure, and epistemic injustice. By staging the poetic voice as witness and the melting Arctic as violated subject, *Arkhticós Dolorôs* articulates “the right to be cold” not as a speculative legal claim, but as an ontological necessity tied to Indigenous sovereignty, memory, and continuity. Through linguistic fragmentation and sensory immersion, Kleemann’s work mirrors the breakdown of both climate and legal language, resisting Western ecological romanticism while indicting the inadequacy of international legal frameworks. What emerges is a decolonial poetics of testimony—less a petition for recognition than an accusation against systems that render such rights unimaginable. In this way, Kleemann drafts a form of “poetic law,” where mourning becomes method and coldness becomes both condition and demand.

Keywords The right to be cold · Arctic · Indigenous testimony · Epistemology of law · Greenland

The phrase “the right to be cold” has come to signify more than a juridical innovation in climate governance. It names a fundamental challenge to how law conceptualizes harm, responsibility, and voice in a warming world. First articulated in transnational human-rights discourse—most prominently in Sheila Watt-Cloutier’s petition to the Inter-American Commission on Human Rights—the claim sought to link Arctic ice loss to the erosion of Indigenous lifeways and to render climate change legible as a human rights violation. Yet the “right to be cold” remains defined

M. H. Birkhold (✉)
Ohio State University, Columbus, OH, USA
e-mail: birkhold.22@osu.edu

A. Juster (ed.), *Legal Drafts in Anthropocene Literature*, SpringerBriefs in Law,
https://doi.org/10.1007/978-3-032-27283-6_5

as much by its failure as by its force. Law demands evidence, causation, and translation: epistemic forms that falter when confronted with slow violence, planetary interdependence, and injuries that exceed human scale. The Arctic could be spoken about, but it could not yet be heard by the law.

This chapter begins from that juridical impasse. Rather than asking how the "right to be cold" might be successfully formalized within existing legal frameworks, it explores what kinds of imagination become possible once we attend to the limits of law's epistemology itself. To pursue this question, the chapter turns to the work of Greenlandic poet and performance artist Jessie Kleemann, whose poetry collection *Arkhticós Dolorôs* (2021) reconfigures the failed legal claim as a form of poetic testimony. Originally performed in 2019 at Blue Lake as part of the *At the Moraine* project, the work emerged from Kleemann's sustained engagement with glacier melt and what the project describes as the "distinct language of the ice, the dying glacier".[1] Kleemann does not write law, argue policy, or seek legal recognition. Yet her work exposes the epistemic assumptions that structure legal knowing and the representational thresholds at which law fails.

The core claim of this chapter is that *Arkhticós Dolorôs* reimagines testimony at three decisive levels. First, it reconceives the Arctic not as an object of protection but as a rights-bearing subject whose injuries cannot be reduced to human loss. Second, it reframes responsibility through what I call global enmeshment, dissolving the territorial and causal boundaries on which jurisdiction conventionally depends. Third, it asks whether another form of legality—a law adequate to the unknown—might emerge from practices that do not presume full comprehension. Kleemann's multilingual, partially opaque poetics thus does not supplement law with feeling; it stages an encounter with the conditions under which legal knowledge itself is produced.

Methodologically, the chapter reads *Arkhticós Dolorôs* not as an intentional legal intervention but as a critical reorganization of law's imaginative terrain. Kleemann's practice embodies the tension of being both Indigenous and "cosmopolitan European," revealing the ambivalence of speaking from within and beyond colonial structures.[2] Unlike the poetry of asylum seekers, for example, who "deliberately insert the literary into the legal order," Kleemann's work is not explicitly juridical; it instead recreates the imaginative conditions under which law apprehends harm and voice.[3] Writing as an Inuit woman, and alternating between Greenlandic, Danish, and English, she stages for many readers a poetics of partial understanding, a practice that asks them to listen even where full comprehension remains impossible.

This multilingual layering reflects what Kirsten Thisted has described as the ambivalence of Greenlandic "blubber poetics," in which languages interpenetrate, producing pride and pain, innovation and loss at once.[4] In their reading of Kleemann's

---

[1] Boetzkes and Diamanti (2020), p. 236.

[2] Ibid.

[3] Reed and Hayes Laughton (2023), p. 554.

[4] Thisted (2017), pp. 286–290.

poem "Eskimothertongue," Ann-Sofie Gremaud and Thisted show how the text dramatizes the impossibility of linguistic purity in a postcolonial Greenlandic setting, turning hybridity into both burden and source of aesthetic creativity.[5] As Thisted has argued more broadly, such linguistic and cultural entanglements are inseparable from Greenland's colonial history and contemporary negotiations of Indigeneity.[6] As a beginning student of Greenlandic, I approach Kleemann's work from within this asymmetry, acknowledging that my own limited access can itself be analyzed as part of the poem's intended structure of address. Across the sections that follow, I argue that *Arkhticós Dolorôs* reconceives testimony itself by demanding precisely this ethically charged posture of partial understanding.

The argument proceeds in five parts. Part 1 reconstructs the emergence—and juridical failure—of the "right to be cold," tracing how the Inuit petition reframed climate change as a human rights issue while colliding with entrenched doctrines of evidence, causation, and jurisdiction. Part 2 introduces Jessie Kleemann and situates *Arkhticós Dolorôs* within her broader artistic practice and Arctic cultural history. Part 3 offers a close reading of the poems' construction of the Arctic as a suffering subject—cold itself as claimant—thereby shifting the right to be cold from a derivative human interest to a more-than-human demand. Part 4 examines how the collection dissolves territorial jurisdiction through its insistence on planetary enmeshment, redistributing responsibility across linguistic, ecological, and geopolitical networks. Part 5 turns to language as law's epistemic foundation, arguing that Kleemann's refusal of full intelligibility models a jurisprudence capable of working with opacity, uncertainty, and the limits of understanding.

Taken together, these readings suggest that the enduring value of the "right to be cold" lies less in its unrealized enforceability than in its capacity to expose the limits of legal imagination. *Arkhticós Dolorôs* does not propose new doctrine. It proposes a different stance: one that treats partial knowledge not as failure but as condition. In doing so, Kleemann's poetry invites us to consider whether justice in the Anthropocene might require not only new rights, but new ways of listening.

1 The Right to Be Cold

In 2005, a novel petition was filed before the Inter-American Commission for Human Rights (IACHR) seeking relief from human rights violations resulting from global warming caused by acts and omissions of the United States. Submitted by Sheila Watt-Cloutier with the support of the Inuit Circumpolar Conference on behalf of all Inuit of the Arctic Regions of the United States and Canada, the first-of-its-kind petition argued that climate change had impacted Inuit rights to culture, property, traditional land, subsistence, housing, health, life, integrity, and security of

[5] Gremaud and Thisted (2020), p. 329.

[6] Thisted (2025), p. 171.

Inuit communities. The arguments came to be encapsulated as "the right to be cold," the principle that Arctic Indigenous peoples have a fundamental right to maintain their traditional way of life, cultural identity, and environment, which depend on the preservation of cold climates and sea ice.[7]

Specifically, the petitioners argued that the United States had breached its obligations under international law by neglecting to cut its greenhouse gas emissions, refusing to participate meaningfully in global climate initiatives, and spreading climate denial that downplayed the urgency of global warming. They asked the IACHR to investigate these charges, hold the United States accountable, and recommend measures to lower emissions while safeguarding Inuit rights, resources, and cultural survival in the face of climate change.[8] The Inuit petition presented a set of novel legal arguments that sought, for the first time, to hold a state responsible for the human rights impacts of climate change.

To substantiate these allegations, the petitioners relied on a variety of forms of evidence, including scientific studies, government reports, oral testimonies and Inuit knowledge (*Inuit Qaujimajatuqangit*, or IQ). Citing the United Nation's Intergovernmental Panel on Climate Change's Third Assessment Report from 2001, for instance, the petition offered graphical evidence of global surface temperature rise.[9] Reports like the U.S. General Accounting Office report *Flooding and Erosion in Alaska Native Villages* were used to show ill effects of climate change, demonstrating how 86% of Alaska Native Villages were already affected by the loss of permafrost and sea ice which removes natural coastal defenses, leading to storm surges, erosion, and land slumping that threaten Inuit homes, cultural sites, and food storage practices.[10] The petition summarized IQ, which tells "the Inuit that the weather is not just warmer in the Arctic, but the entire familiar landscape is metamorphosing into an unknown land".[11] Further, oral testimony such as that offered by Barrow resident Ronald Brower offered evocative examples of adversities: "The climatic changes, especially the changes to our ocean, are affecting our ability to feed our families.... We're not catching as many spring whales as we used to".[12] By combining these various forms of evidence and including Indigenous voices, the petition sought to show that the Inuit are reliant on the cold to survive, and that the cold is disappearing.

Ultimately, the innovative reframing of climate change as a human rights problem was declared inadmissible by the IACHR. After a year, the Commission responded in a two-paragraph letter explaining that the petition could not be processed because "the information provided does not enable us to determine whether the alleged facts would tend to characterize a violation of rights protected by the

[7] Cf. Watt-Cloutier (2015).

[8] Cf. ibid., p. 118.

[9] Cf. Petition (2001), pp. 21–22.

[10] Cf. ibid., p. 51.

[11] Ibid., p. 21.

[12] Ibid., p. 66.

American Declaration [the IACHR 2006]" (Decision, np). The law, in short, did not know what to make of the petition.

Existing legal frameworks struggle to accommodate the claims raised by Sheila Watt-Cloutier. Human rights law is traditionally structured around the identification of discrete violations, attributable to specific state conduct, and accompanied by enforceable remedies. Climate change, however, has traditionally resisted this doctrinal framework.[13] The harms it produces—melting sea ice, coastal erosion, disruptions to subsistence economies—are cumulative, diffuse, and transboundary, rendering it exceedingly difficult to establish causation and attribution to a particular state in a manner that satisfies adjudicatory thresholds.[14] Consequently, as the Office of the United Nations High Commissioner for Human Rights has observed, the physical impacts of global warming cannot readily be classified as human rights violations precisely because they cannot be directly traced to the acts or omissions of identifiable states.[15] Even assuming such attribution could be demonstrated, the governing corpus of international human rights treaties is territorially bounded, concerned primarily with the relationship between a government and the people under its jurisdiction. It therefore provides little doctrinal basis for imposing extraterritorial obligations upon states whose emissions contribute to harms experienced beyond their borders. For this reason, critiques in environmental law scholarship consistently underscore the *justiciability gap* inherent in claims like the "right to be cold."[16] The right lacks recognition in core human rights instruments, enjoys no settled status in customary international law, and is underdeveloped with respect to state obligations. Attempts to litigate climate harms as human rights violations thus collide with structural legal constraints: evidentiary burdens of causation, jurisdictional limits of treaty bodies, and the absence of clear remedial standards.

Yet, "the right to be cold" has proven an influential concept that has helped reframe climate change as a human rights problem. Many now understand the phrase, even if the law does not. As Sébastien Jodoin, Shannon Snow, and Arielle Corobow observe, "At a time when climate governance was primarily understood as a technical issue connected to scientific projections, economic valuations, and legalistic language, the petition articulated a novel 'climate rights' frame that, like the broader climate justice frame, emphasizes the moral dimensions of climate change by stressing its costs and consequences for particular communities and bringing to

[13] Courts are beginning to stretch or adapt this framework. In *Saúl Luciano Lliuya v. RWE*, for example, the Higher Regional Court of Hamm (OLG Hamm) recognized the possibility of legal responsibility for climate-related harm despite a spatial and causal disconnection between the source of emissions and the materialization of harm across national borders.

[14] A growing body of scholarship arguing for environmentalism to be part of human rights and analyzing the obstacles. For example, Pelizzon (2019), p. 99, criticizes the systems that make damage to the earth and its ecosystems "legally irrelevant"; Bosselmann (2017) argues for an ecological approach to human rights based on the interdependence of rights and duties; Wewerinke-Singh (2019) identifies new potentials in rights-based climate actions; Hiskes (2009).

[15] Cf. Report (2009), par. 70.

[16] For example, Knox (2009), pp. 477–498.

the forefront the voices of marginalized communities".[17] In this respect, the "right to be cold" has succeeded in reshaping the discourse about the cold, even if it has faltered as a claim within the formal structures of human rights law.

Still, the gap between influence and enforceability makes clear the limits of the legal imagination. The value of human rights law lies not only in providing remedies for past violations but also in supplying a set of internationally agreed values that can motivate collective action and help shape more robust responses.[18] To the extent the "right to be cold" has value, it is because it unsettles conventional categories and exposes the inability of human rights doctrine to capture the experience of climate harm. The next section turns to the Greenlandic artist Jessie Kleemann, whose work does not offer a policy prescription or promote a "forward-looking framework" in the manner of law and governance, but instead mounts an implicit critique of law's conceptual boundaries and its failures of recognition. Through her art, Kleemann helps us imagine legal futures that depart from the strictures of enforceability and jurisdiction, challenging us to consider how law itself might be reconfigured in the face of a warming world.

2 Jessie Kleemann & *Arkhticós Dolorôs*

Over the past several decades, Jessie Kleemann has established herself as an eminent contemporary voice from Greenland. Born in Upernavik in 1959, she trained first at the Tuukkaq Theatre in Denmark and later returned to Nuuk, where she became director of the Graphic Workshop in the 1980s. Since then, Kleemann has worked across performance, installation, and poetry while building networks with other Indigenous artists in the Arctic and beyond. Her artistic trajectory is marked by a deep engagement with questions of cultural survival, decolonization, and environmental transformation.

Kleemann's work often takes Greenland's rapidly changing climate as a central subject, using artistic form to register both ecological and cultural shifts. Installations such as *The Sledge on the Way* (2023) at the Statens Museum for Kunst in Denmark, for instance, highlight the fragility of traditional tools and practices under the pressures of global warming, inviting contemplation about obsolesce, evolution, and continuities with Greenlandic heritage. In other works, she employs slow, deliberate movements and gestures that recall her background in theatre, allowing her performances to meditate on time, endurance, and loss. Her poetry collection *Arkhticós Dolorôs* (2021), nominated for the Nordic Council Literature Prize, extends this inquiry by staging the Arctic as both a place of pain and resilience, foregrounding the embodied consequences of environmental change.

---

[17] Jodoin et al. (2020), p. 173.

[18] Cf. Limon (2009), pp. 439–440.

Kleemann's art speaks to a desire not simply to protect a landscape of ice and snow, but to defend a way of life from which climate, culture, and identity are inseparable. Her performances remind audiences that melting ice is not only a scientific metric or global policy issue but also a lived reality for Indigenous communities whose histories have long been shaped by colonialism and marginalization.[19] In this sense, Kleemann's art speaks simultaneously to Greenland's specific conditions and to wider Arctic struggles for recognition, cultural continuity, and environmental justice. Annelis Kuhlmann observes that discussions of Greenlandic performance cannot be disentangled from questions of climate and colonialism.[20] Kleemann's practice embodies this entanglement. By staging Greenland in both Danish and international contexts, she exposes the paradoxes of postcolonial representation, where formal independence coexists with enduring colonial attitudes and exclusions. Her work intervenes in this tension by insisting on Greenlandic perspectives, reclaiming Indigenous presence in spaces where it has often been muted. While doing so, she challenges audiences to rethink the cultural and political stakes of a warming Arctic.[21] In doing so, Kleemann transforms stages and galleries into sites where art becomes inseparable from the right to climate, culture, and equality.

Jessie Kleemann's *Arkhticós Dolorôs* emerged from a workshop within the research project *At the Moraine: Envisioning the Concerns of Ice*, held in Ilulissat, Greenland, in 2019. Conceived initially as a video performance before becoming a poetry collection with the same title, the work extends Kleemann's long-standing engagement with Greenland's melting ice and colonial histories. On the project's website, she is described as a "project partner" whose performances create "a visceral sense of Arctic landscapes as they are embodied through myth, voice, sound, and movement."[22] Her contribution sought to render a sensory experience of the UNESCO-protected glacier *Sermeq Kujalleq*, translating its slow violence into corporeal gesture and sound. The title explicitly alludes to Barry Lopez's *Arctic Dreams* (1986), where *Arkticós* denotes a special "Arctic quality," an attitude of reverence toward the northern world. Yet Kleemann reworks Lopez's vision: if his *Arkticós* gestures toward a Western recovery of awe and respect, her *Arkhticós* insists instead on embodiment, vulnerability, and contradiction, on what Kirsten Thisted calls "a suffering Arctic" caught between colonial modernity and ecological precarity.[23] Where Lopez finds in the Arctic a route back to premodern wholeness, Kleemann locates fracture, contamination, and care within a resolutely modern and mediated terrain.

Kleemann's *Arkhticós Dolorôs* invents its own language—an interwoven fabric of Greenlandic, Danish, English, and fragments of others—that resists seamless

[19] Norman (2018), p. 149.

[20] Kuhlmann (2017).

[21] Norman argues that Kleemann's "embodied practice"—informed by traditional Kalaallit performance, analog video, and ecopoetic forms—relocates the body as a site of knowledge and ethical agency, especially "environmental collapse." Norman (2022), pp. 30–43.

[22] Available at https://atthemoraine.com/abstracts/arkhticos-doloros/.

[23] Thisted (2025), p. 171.

translation. Thisted notes that Kleemann's poetry "can only be fully grasped by those familiar with the respective languages," yet this very untranslatability becomes the work's central aesthetic force, rendering visible the linguistic and cultural fissures that structure contemporary Greenlandic life.[24] And Greenlandic performance, as Annelis Kuhlmann observes, cannot be separated from questions of climate and colonialism ("Performing Greenland"). By fusing Catholic iconography (Nuestra Señora de los Dolores), Indigenous cosmology (Sassuma Arnaa), and contemporary ecological anxiety, Kleemann forges a new mythic register to stage these entanglements. The result is a poetics of estrangement: language becomes glacial, layered, and partially opaque, inviting the reader to inhabit the gap between comprehension and sensation.

The following section turns from the performance and its multimedia genesis to a close reading of the poetry collection itself. By examining *Arkhticós Dolorôs* as a text rather than an event, this chapter explores how Kleemann's language performs the limits of understanding and what it might mean to read for the ungraspable. If *Arkhticós Dolorôs* creates a linguistic landscape that eludes full interpretation by many readers, this elusiveness becomes integral to its ethical force: it asks how one might apprehend the Arctic—and its pain—without claiming mastery over it. At the heart of Kleemann's art lies the probing question Inuit activist Sheila Watt-Cloutier has framed as the right to be cold: the right to maintain a climate, a culture, and a continuity of life inseparable from the frozen world.

3 A Subject in Pain

Sheila Watt-Cloutier's petition before the Inter-American Commission on Human Rights sought to translate melting ice into a register the law could hear. Its polyvocal brief assembled climate data, witness statements, and community testimony to show how changing ice and snow conditions threatened Inuit safety, health, and culture. But in trying to satisfy the evidentiary form of a legal document, that testimony was also constrained by it. Rendered in the idiom of proof, the voices of the petitioners could not establish the "right to be cold" as a legally recognizable claim. The document demonstrated that the Arctic could be spoken about but could not speak for itself. Jessie Kleemann's *Arkhticós Dolorôs* takes up precisely this foundering, transforming the question of representation into one of testimony. Her poetry does not translate experience into evidence; it reimagines what it means to testify from, and for, the Arctic itself. Through her multilingual, formally fractured, and sensorially charged language, Kleemann constructs a poetics that both extends and critiques the legal petition. Her work helps us to conceive the Arctic as a rights-bearing being whose injuries demand a new form of witnessing; to locate responsibility within a web of global enmeshment that dissolves jurisdictional borders; and,

[24] Ibid.

finally, to confront the limits of juridical knowledge by imagining a law capable of working with the unknown. If Watt-Cloutier's petition sought recognition through intelligibility, Kleemann's poems make recognition possible only through estrangement—through the act of listening to what cannot be fully understood.

Though Sheila Watt-Cloutier's petition before the Inter-American Commission on Human Rights translated melting ice into a legal harm, the "right to be cold" remains legally unrecognized in core international treaties and conceptually confined to human injury. Jessie Kleemann's *Arkhticós Dolorôs* moves this claim to a different register, abstracting and intensifying it as she transforms climate injury into bodily pain experienced by the Arctic itself. In so doing, her poetry articulates what others have called a poetics of environmental personhood, in which the cryosphere becomes a subject of suffering and a claimant of rights.[25]

The collection collapses the boundary between human body and Arctic ground, animating the landscape and conferring a kind of selfhood upon it. Midway through the collection, a poem begins, "*min jord i Arktis er" [my earth in the Arctic is].*[26] *In Greenlandic, the speaker continues "issittumi nunap issualtassa uanga issora*" *[At the edge of the Arctic land/that is my origin], before switching to English, "soil on Arctic lands/it is as you know my body of soil"*.[27] The triple apposition—earth/soil/body—transforms the space into a subject. The poem then names the body: "*arkhticos/(hvor doloro og doloros) er*," situating pain (*dolor*) within "the Arctic" as a proper name. This resounds in the early work of Julie Cruikshank, who showed how Indigenous Arctic knowledge understands glaciers as responsive social actors, and how these epistemologies challenge colonial histories and modern scientific and legal frameworks that treat ice as inert matter rather than as an agent embedded in social and moral relations (*Do Glaciers Listen?* 2005).

The body Kleemann's poetry presents, however, is further personified through the evocation of the "*kuldevæsen*" [cold-being].[28] The poem initially questions our perceptual capabilities, "*det hvider og gør dig blind*" [it whitens and makes you

[25] Over the past decade, debates in environmental law and the environmental humanities have increasingly shifted from metaphorical invocations of nature toward sustained legal and philosophical arguments for recognizing nonhuman entities as rights-bearing subjects. Recent scholarship no longer treats environmental personhood as a speculative gesture but as a response to the structural limits of anthropocentric environmental regulation, drawing on constitutional reforms, judicial decisions, and Indigenous legal frameworks. Alexandra Juster's contribution to this volume offers a particularly synthetic account of these developments by reading Jean Giono's *The Man, who Planted Trees* (1999 [1953]) as an early literary articulation of bio-centric legal thinking, linking critical nature writing, Indigenous cosmologies, and contemporary rights-of-nature jurisprudence. Her analysis situates the attribution of legal subjectivity to nature within a broader framework of stewardship and fiduciary responsibility, anticipating current legal debates about environmental personhood and guardianship models. For broader legal and public-facing reflections on the recognition of nature as a legal subject, see also Weydt (2023), which documents recent cases in which animals, rivers, forests, and ecosystems appear as claimants before courts, and Gordon (2018).

[26] Kleemann (2021), p. 49.

[27] Ibid. Translations mine unless otherwise noted.

[28] Ibid., p. 56.

blind] such that we are unsure of what we see "sort sne og havet hvidt i/gråt og rødt hvilken farve er det" [black snow and the sea white in/grey and red what color is that], but places the being squarely if questioningly in planetary terms, "*dette noget I en lille blå planet?*" [*is it something on a little blue planet?*"].[29] Cold is more than a number on a thermometer. The *kuldevæsen* is rendered addressable. "*hun/fryser i saltet/i den tynde luft*," [she/freezes in the salt/in the thin air].[30] The poem begins by gendering cold ("she") and placing her in precise media—salt, thin air—through which light and life circulate. The poetic language describes the cold as a body, too: snow that "*bløder og smelter*" [bleeds and melts].[31]

Throughout, the reader, pulled into the grammatical community created by the text, witnesses and intercedes, not to domesticate the Arctic, but to acknowledge: "*Her hvor vi varmer den i blikket/Vi ser dig kuldevæsen*" [Here where we warm it in the gaze/we see you, cold-being].[32] The poem describes a reciprocal visibility: we warm "her" with our gaze even as we see her. By naming *arkhticos* and *kuldevæsen*, Kleemann supplies stable, repeatable subjects of address. The Arctic is not "like" a person; it is a being with a name, a body ("my body of soil"), and sensations: "*kuldevæsens smerte knager*" [pain creaks].[33] There is new ontological specification.

The Arctic is a being, teeming with life. Throughout the arkhticós sequence,[34] the world is not scenery but sensorium: "*livet er mikroskpopisk forbundet med/solens hurtige skift til langsomme sorte og blå vinternætter der rækker/langt ind I foråret og*" [life is microscopically connected to/the sun's rapid shifts into slow black and blue winter nights that reach/far into the spring and] and then "*så sommeren I evigt flux/hvor blåklokken viser sig end ag eller to gennem en revne på klippen*" [so the summer in eternal flux/where the bluebell appears once or twice through a crack in the rock].[35] The bluebell's brief emergence marks time the way a pulse does, as if the Arctic's capillaries were briefly visible.

In the cosmology presented by the poems, the various organisms, including algae, roots, and ice, are beings whose ongoing existence constitutes part of a larger whole. This collective body encompasses the human and nonhuman alike. "*Mine mennesker fryser/De er billedet på mig/Jeg er arkhtikós/Og ikke alene*" [My people are freezing/They are the image of me/I am Arkhtikós/and not alone].[36] Here, identification flows both ways: humans mirror the Arctic, and the Arctic mirrors them. Coldness becomes kinship. The juridical concept of "environmental harm" presumes an external object like land, air, or sea is damaged in ways that subsequently affect people. Kleemann reverses this causality. The harm begins in the Arctic's own

[29] Ibid.

[30] Ibid., p. 58.

[31] Ibid., p. 56.

[32] Ibid., p. 58.

[33] Ibid., p. 56.

[34] Ibid., pp. 49–59.

[35] Ibid., p. 50.

[36] Ibid., p. 59.

body: snow that bleeds, light that dims, algae that die. Human suffering enters not as metaphor but as symptom of a larger being in pain.

Indeed, this Arctic is in pain, not as a metaphor but as a state of existence. "*Arkhticós dolorôs*." The snow "bleeds," it does not just melt. Something is wrong. Early, the lyrical speaker states: "*tallene stiller pilene ned/kan vi lave en graf*" [the numbers point the arrows downward/can we make a graph].[37] The question reads as both parody and refusal: can we graph pain, quantify melt, render testimony in metrics admissible to law? Fifty pages later, after describing a variety of harms from melting to sea level rise, a sort of answer arrives: "*vi kommer til at være døve I stormen*" [we will be deaf in the storm].[38] Between these lines stretches an epistemological chasm. Law listens for data, but Kleemann's Arctic speaks through sounds as well as silences and spaces.

Kleeman stages melting formally, on the page, by turning *white space itself into ice*—a material that expands, fractures, and finally thins to near-absence. At the beginning of the collection, white space functions as structural mass: gaps between words and lines create distance, opacity, and resistance, mimicking the solidity and accumulation of ice. This logic reaches an extreme in the eighth poem, where spacing collapses altogether. The absence of white space produces a dense, pressurized textual block, akin to ice compacted under force—no breath, no separation, no room for movement. Language here freezes into a single, continuous surface.[39] As the collection progresses, this density gives way to loss and dispersal. White space returns not as structure but as absence. In the final poems, the page opens up, with language reduced to fragments surrounded by emptiness. The poem on page 89—two words, *"kom/her," [come/here]* suspended between wide blank intervals—enacts the final stage of melting: matter thinned to trace, presence reduced to a gesture or call. What once filled the page now recedes, leaving voids where language—and ice—used to be. In this way, Kleeman does not merely describe melting; she performs it typographically. The reader experiences thaw as a visual and temporal process: compression, cracking, and finally dispersal. Blank space becomes an index of loss and a fragile summons to witness it.

In Kleemann's poetics, quantification gives way to sensation. For instance, in expressions like "*altså vandet slår og slår og slår på klippen*" [so the water strikes and strikes and strikes the rock],[40] the repetition performs a material testimony that cannot be charted but can be felt by the reader. Where climate reports translate damage into charts and percentages, *Arkhticós Dolorôs* translates damage into affect, sound, and embodied resonance. Its evidentiary mode is lyric rather than forensic: pain is not necessarily *proved* but felt and *heard and experienced through the act of reading*. In juridical terms, the poems grant the Arctic its own *injury-in-fact*,

[37] Ibid., p. 11.

[38] Ibid., p. 61.

[39] Ibid., pp. 12–13.

[40] Ibid., p. 16.

concrete, particularized, and actual harms. Warming is thus not just environmental change; it is an assault on the integrity of a being.

By merging ecological and human pain, Kleemann exposes the inadequacy of rights frameworks that compartmentalize injury. Her poetry refuses the legal fiction that separates person from environment. "*I am arkhticós/And not alone*"[41] discloses a condition of shared embodiment that law has only begun to recognize. To injure the Arctic is to injure its people, not symbolically but ontologically. This fusion recasts Watt-Cloutier's "right to be cold" as a more-than-human claim, one that demands a juridical imagination capable of hearing what the graphs cannot communicate: the voice of the cold-being itself.

The force of Kleemann's intervention is thus to move the "right to be cold" from a derivative human interest (humans harmed by warming) to a primary claim voiced by cold itself. If personhood in law is, at bottom, a technology for recognizing subjects who can be harmed and can claim reparation, then *Arkhticós Dolorôs* rehearses the prerequisites of such recognition: named subject, felt harm, articulated norm. The sequence does not deny human witness—"*Her hvor vi varmer den i blikket*"—but it decouples witness from proprietorship. The Arctic becomes the rights-bearer itself. Kleemann therefore stages, through poetic speech, the precise scene where legal imagination stops, and where another kind of standing begins.

4 Global Enmeshment and the Unbounded Jurisdiction of the Arctic

To hold someone or something accountable for violations of the "right to be cold" requires a different conception of responsibility—one unbounded by the territorial logic of jurisdiction.[42] *Global enmeshment* names this condition: a structural and material entanglement of ecological, economic, atmospheric, linguistic, and affective systems in which actions in one site are constitutively linked to consequences elsewhere, without clear spatial, temporal, or juridical boundaries. It describes not mere interconnection but a dense mesh of reciprocal implication, where extraction, combustion, circulation, and representation bind distant actors into shared climatic outcomes. *Arkhticós Dolorôs* performs precisely this reconceptualization. Across its multilingual and multisensory field, Kleemann's text exposes how every breath, sound, and extraction in the global system reverberates in the Arctic. Her poems insist on interdependence, whether economic, linguistic, meteorological, affective, so that responsibility can no longer be contained within national borders or measured by conventional chains of causation. The Arctic does not lie at the world's edge but at its center, where the effects of global action manifest most visibly and painfully.

[41] Ibid., p. 59.

[42] Cf. Antoniazzi (2024).

Kleemann explicitly collapses the boundaries that law and colonial governance once assumed. Traditional frameworks fail:

er der et kort
et rutekort på landevejen
eller henover isfjeldenes lag af moræne din gps under strømledningen
så har du måske svaret
ikke
eller ikke svaret

[is there a map
a route map on the highway
or across the icebergs' layers of moraine your GPS under the power line
then perhaps you have the answer
not
or not the answer][43]

The way to make sense of this Arctic space is through charted space. "*qualaaniit inqquneq isigalugu from a birdseye perspective så er vi alle hernede*" [Seen from a bird's-eye view of the qualaaniit's entanglement, we are all here below].[44] The perspective of the qualaaniit, meaning outsiders or Europeans, is distorting. The poems continues: "*inuit allat/kalaallit qallunaat de grønlandske danskere som virkelig er/ de andre/også de andre/the others/soorlu uagut*" [Inuit—all of them/ Kalaallit, qallunaat, the Greenlandic Danes who truly are the Others/also the others/the others/ just like us].[45] The refrain "like us" erases the distance between observer and object, replacing jurisdictional separation with a sort of ethical adjacency, *a relational orientation that insists on proximity without assimilation, cultivating responsibility through shared exposure.*[46] This global togetherness is not necessarily harmonious; it is a condition of entanglement through shared vulnerability and complicity. It is part of what must be unlearned, "is there a mathematical system to be learned or unlearned?".[47]

In this redefined jurisdiction, causality here is not linear but circulatory:

"*havet vil stige*
ikke herfra men længere nede fra subarctic arctic"

[the sea will rise
not from here but farther down, from the subarctic Arctic].[48]

The line break and spatial separation enact the poem's claim that causality does not originate "here" but elsewhere, visually displacing agency and forcing the reader to experience harm as something deferred, distributed, and circulating across

---

[43] Kleemann (2021), p. 45.

[44] Ibid., p. 45.

[45] Ibid.

[46] For a discussion see: Link and Lewis (2025). The idea of adjacency comes from: Campt (2023).

[47] Ibid.

[48] Ibid., p. 61.

spatial systems rather than emanating from a single, local source. Harm, though felt in the Arctic, is redefined as something that moves through interlocking systems of atmosphere, ocean, and land. No single site can be isolated from the planetary flows of damage and accountability.

Language itself becomes a medium of this unbounded jurisdiction. Midway through the collection, the poems shift into English, opening the Arctic's voice to a different international audience. "The universe is not ending lee, we all love you/as you love all/and love us," Kleemann writes, followed by the line "the refugees fleeing the war everything's getting closer/it is not only the water rising taking away hope as if/the ice shedding ice/shake things on earth".[49] The poem expands Arctic suffering into a planetary register where melting, migration, and militarization converge. The subsequent poem, beginning "WE HAVE TOO MUCH FEAR," lists nation-states—"US, Russia, Turkey, Iran, France, Germany, Denmark, Sweden, Norway, Korea, Japan"[50]—rendering visible the geopolitical network whose extractive activities have violated the cold being's rights. Through this enumeration, Kleemann transforms poetic space into a kind jurisdictional space, a global ledger of responsibility.

Temporal as well as spatial boundaries collapse. "*hver dag er en umulig rejse gennem vinteren iglootelte eller/human sult og en sikker langsom død kommer nummer kommer båd/kommer tog gennem den globale Verdens tikken*" ["every day is an impossible journey through the winter igloo tents or/human hunger and a certain slow death comes number comes boat/comes train through the global World's ticking].[51] Here, the Arctic becomes a node in the metronomic rhythm of global time, caught in the ticking of modernity's clock. Responsibility, in this framework, must likewise be temporalized globally; accountability cannot be limited to the moment of emission, decision, or event.

Later, the poem explicitly shifts from describing Arctic crisis to interrogating existing modes of organizing planetary space and territoriality:

moder arktis lidelse
er det den nye medsmeltnings istid
nu åbnes for en krigstid for de nye efterkommere
hvem ejer Jorden
skal vi sige ingen ejer Jorden
så hvorfor forsvare eller være imod
at sælge den så pludseligt
og til hvem

[mother Arctic's suffering
is this the new age of co-melting ice
now a time of war opens for the new descendants
who owns the Earth
shall we say no one owns the Earth

---

[49] Ibid., p. 42.
[50] Ibid., p. 43.
[51] Ibid., p. 46.

so why defend it or be against
selling it so suddenly
and to whom].[52]

The passage questions not only ownership itself but the gestures of control (defending, selling, protecting) that underwrite extractive sovereignty. The poem concludes with a call to awaken from "the evil dream" (*"vi sover I den onde drøm"*) "unlesswefighttowakeup" (*"medmindrevikæmperforatvågneop"*),[53] demanding new imaginaries of stewardship and belonging. The collapsing of spaces in the final phrase ("medmindrevikæmperforatvågneop") visually enacts the collapse of distance, a compressing thought, action, and urgency into a single, breathless unit that stages awakening not as reflection but as an immediate, collective struggle that can no longer afford pauses, separations, or the distinctive jurisdictions. In this way, *Arkhticós Dolorôs* transforms the Arctic from a passive site of observation into an active forum of accountability. It invites a jurisprudence adequate to a planet in motion, one capable of hearing claims that emerge "through the global World's ticking" and of recognizing that the law's jurisdiction is not bounded by the state but coextensive with the earth itself.

5 Toward a Law of Unknowns

Through its multilingual poetics, including acts of translation, untranslatability, and refusal, Kleemann's *Arkhticós Dolorôs* reframes the "right to be cold" not only as a matter of responsibility but as a problem of knowability. Read in light of the Inuit's novel legal claim, her language makes us confront the limits of juridical knowledge and evidentiary form. Since language is the epistemic foundation of law, law is not grounded in coercion or facts alone, but in linguistically mediated rules and interpretive practices.[54] Accordingly, legal meaning exists only within interpretive linguistic communities.[55] What can law know, and what does it do when confronted with what it cannot? But what if the law cannot fully comprehend the language its subject speaks? The poems refuse the premise that all injury must be rendered intelligible. Instead, they stage an epistemology of cold that exposes the epistemic violence implicit in law's demand for clarity. To modify Julie Stone Peters's description of narrative jurisprudence as a "cure through its access to a previously inaccessible reality," Kleemann's cure lies precisely in *withholding* such access.[56] Her storytell-

[52] Ibid., p. 52.

[53] Ibid.

[54] This insight has long been central to legal theory, particularly in traditions that understand law as a practice of interpretation rather than mere command or facticity, emphasizing how meaning, normativity, and authority emerge through language itself. For foundational texts, see: White (1973); Dworkin (1986); Hart (1994).

[55] Fish (1982), p. 558.

[56] Peters (2005), p. 447.

ing does not uncover a hidden truth; it insists that knowledge itself has become glacial: slow, layered, and refracted through the prism of the perspective through which one sees it. Kleeman admits the possibility that some realities might remain partially inaccessible.

Throughout the collection, the Arctic, the cold—this new subject—is rendered into language. The poems themselves repeatedly call attention to this process of representation. The poems' oscillation between Greenlandic, Danish, and English mirrors the wavering between what can and cannot be known. While Kleemann's multilingual verse exemplifies "translanguaging," a practice that unsettles linguistic hierarchy and mirrors Greenland's colonial entanglement, Ushma Chauhan Jacobsen notes, the texts explicitly play with accessibility and inaccessibility.[57] Kleemann's endnotes dramatize the uneven conditions of access. The very first footnote appears to promise transparency: "*Digtsamlingens tekster er flersproglige. I mange tilfælde gentages de grønlandske linjer på dansk eller omvendt*" [The texts of the poetry collection are multilingual. In many cases, the Greenlandic lines are repeated in Danish or vice versa].[58] But this assurance immediately unravels. The promise is that "in many cases" not "all" the lines are repeated in the corresponding language. In practice, the Greenlandic and Danish lines often do not perfectly correspond. The pages simulate symmetry without delivering equivalence. For monolingual readers—especially those who read Danish but not Greenlandic—the text offers only partial access, a mirage of understanding. Those who speak both languages, and who therefore inhabit Greenland's colonial history and its lived Arctic experience, grasp nuances that remain invisible to others. The result is a poetics of differentiated legibility, where comprehension itself becomes a potential form of situated knowledge.

This deliberate partiality transforms reading into an ethical act. The reader, or a reader who does not understand Greenlandic, is positioned, like the judge in an impossible case, before testimony they cannot fully decode. The multilingual weave turns the audience into what Yoko Tawada calls an exophonic subject—someone reading from the outside, aware of dependence, loss, and the materiality of language itself.[59] The experience is not failure but method. Just as the law demands translation of every harm into a common metric, Kleemann refuses to translate suffering into a single idiom. Meaning must remain multiple, provisional, and sometimes inaccessible. The gaps on the page—the irregular spacing, the white fields between verses—perform both ice and ignorance: the material whiteness of the Arctic and the epistemic blank of those who presume to know it.

The footnotes amplify this method rather than resolve it. Their glosses gesture toward knowledge: *uniinnartoqassanngilaq*, we learn, is a response to the national

---

[57] Jacobsen (2022), p. 33.

[58] Kleemann (2021), p. 99.

[59] For a new translation of Tawada's meditations on the subject, see: Tawada (2025). For insightful discussions of Tawada's exophony, see: Pajević (2020), pp. 494–504; Wright (2008), pp. 26–42.

poet Henrik Lund;[60] "*Gulligt lys*" [yellow light] refers to the even glow of a blubber lamp;[61] *nunatakker* are land points protruding through ice and also a pun on the Danish *tak* ("thank you," note 12).[62] But these explanations refuse closure. Each gloss opens another layer of mediation, a hinge between oral myth, colonial etymology, and scientific observation. The notes appear to clarify yet continually defer full comprehension, staging the same asymmetry that structures climate governance itself. Kleemann's paratext thus functions as both translation and resistance: it acknowledges the reader's desire for understanding while preserving the opacity that confirms the Arctic's autonomy.

Through this architecture, language becomes law's counterexample. The Greenlandic imperative "*uniinnartoqassanngilaq*" [stopping will not be possible][63] serves as both moral command and linguistic barrier. It resists domestication even as it instructs continuation. When the poem commands, "*frys frys nu til/frys til is vort kuldevæsens sne*" [Freeze, freeze now freeze into ice, our cold-being's snow],[64] the verb form doubles as legislation: it establishes a right and a duty, the right of the cold to persist and the duty of others to ensure it. Where environmental law recognizes glaciers as objects or resources, *Arkhticós Dolorôs* recognizes them as co-subjects whose violation constitutes moral and perhaps legal injury. This refiguration answers Louis Kotzé's critique of the anthropocentric bias of Earth jurisprudence, offering instead a jurisprudence of co-suffering.[65]

The law's evidentiary regime—its dependence on metrics, causation, and transparency—cannot encompass this kind of knowledge. Legal narrativists such as Richard Delgado and for Nancy Levit.[66,67] have argued that storytelling engages conscience, offering affective truth where doctrinal logic fails. Kleemann radicalizes their insight. Her narrative does not aim for empathy through intelligibility but for ethical attention through disorientation. Even orientation fails— "is there a map".[68] To be just is to admit one's lostness. The poem's refusal of cartographic closure parallels its refusal of epistemic closure. The law of unknowns, then, is not a statute but a stance, an acknowledgment that justice in the Anthropocene must learn to operate amid opacity and uncertainty, amid incomplete and imperfect knowledge.

If *Arkhticós Dolorôs* begins by giving voice to the Arctic, it ends by withdrawing certainty from the reader. The poems do not clarify but deepen unknowing:

vi kommer til at grave sne længe

---

[60] Kleemann (2021), note 5.

[61] Ibid., note 11.

[62] Ibid., note 12.

[63] Ibid., p. 11.

[64] Ibid., p. 58.

[65] Cf. Kotzé (2020), pp. 429–430.

[66] Delgado (1989), pp. 2411–2441.

[67] Levit (1997), pp. 389–416.

[68] Kleemann (2021), p. 45.

den grå masse uden næring

vi kommer til at være døve I stormen
som den vi ser på skærmen nu
det sværeste som ingen ved

[we will go on digging snow for a long time
the grey mass without nourishment

we will be deaf in the storm
like the one we are watching on the screen now
the hardest thing, which no one knows].[69]

But in this deafness lies the possibility of another hearing, one attuned not to evidence but to echo, vibration, and pause. Kleemann's poetry teaches that to recognize the Arctic's rights, we must also recognize the limits of our comprehension. A law of unknowns would not overcome ignorance; it would institutionalize humility and non-knowledge.[70] It would listen where understanding fails and finds in the unreadable page the trace of a world still breathing beneath the melt and recognize it as a subject with rights.

6 Conclusion

The right to be cold, then, finds in Kleemann's poetry neither ratification nor rejection but re-creation. If Sheila Watt-Cloutier's petition sought recognition from an existing legal order, *Arkhticós Dolorôs* imagines another. Her poems occupy what might be called the juridical imaginary, a space where law's categories of personhood, harm, and standing are stretched until they recognize each other.[71] Within this

---

[69] Ibid. p. 61.

[70] Some philosophers treat *epistemic humility* as a virtue that arises precisely *from recognizing limits of knowledge and the inevitability of ignorance*. This is directly relevant to framing a law that does not suppress ignorance but *institutionalizes humility toward the unknown*. See Porter et al. (2022). Others have called for a distinction between "ignorance" and "non-knowledge," arguing that the latter is a specific kind of knowledge that should function within regulation and accountability. See, e.g. Paul et al. (2022), pp. 419–432.

[71] Louis J. Kotzé has argued that the Anthropocene should be understood not merely as a descriptive scientific category but as a catalyst for a radical rethinking of global environmental law and governance, one that exposes the inadequacy of existing legal concepts of responsibility, agency, and harm. In calling for a new theoretical foundation capable of supporting comprehensive legal reform, Kotzé emphasizes the need to unsettle established juridical assumptions and to redesign law's processes, priorities, and values in light of human-driven planetary change. It is in this sense that the "juridical imaginary" invoked here may be understood: not as a doctrinal space formally recognized by law, but as an imaginative and critical register in which law's conventional categories of personhood, harm, and standing are pushed to their breaking point, allowing literary and poetic forms to anticipate modes of legal reasoning not yet available within positive law. See Kotzé (2014), pp. 121–156.

space, glaciers speak, algae mourn, and cold itself demands redress. Kleemann transforms the Arctic from the object of legal description into its author, a claimant whose pain both defies and redefines the evidentiary logic that failed the petition.

In place of the procedural and evidentiary rigor of rights-based climate litigation, Kleemann offers a poetics of standing grounded in sensation and interdependence. Her verse performs the transformation that law could not yet enact. It grants the Arctic not representation but voice. Its lines read as a normative appeal, a right articulated by the cold itself: to persist, to be allowed to remain cold. In that plea, poetics and jurisprudence converge. The Arctic's call is not for preservation as property but for recognition as kin.[72]

If Watt-Cloutier's petition asked the law to extend its protection for humans northward, to push environmental law to consider human rights, Kleemann's *Arkhticós Dolorôs* moves the law's horizon altogether. Her poetry models a new kind of legal imagination that is now coming into existence—one capacious enough to admit opacity, nonhuman agency, and the limits of comprehension. One that conceptualizes global enmeshment as rendering existing ideas about territorially bound jurisdiction meaningless. Recent legal developments, from constitutional recognitions of the rights of nature to the attribution of legal subjectivity to rivers, seas, and lakes, suggest that this imagination is no longer confined to theory alone. Yet these juridical experiments remain conceptually fragile, dependent on forms of guardianship and translation that may strain against the very entities they seek to protect. If a river can only act through human proxies who must translate nonhuman injury into forms of harm legible to courts, these new rights preserve anthropocentric structures at the moment of recognition, reinscribing the very frameworks of control and intelligibility that such recognition seeks to unsettle.

To make these advancements robust and lasting, Kleemann's text proposes that justice in the Anthropocene will depend less on new doctrines than on new forms of listening: to silence, to strangeness, to what we do not fully understand. The right to be cold thus becomes not only a legal claim but an epistemic challenge. As Johannes Riquet and Liisa-Rávná Finbog write, Kleemann's poetry "ties together Arctic landscapes and bodies in its reflection on climate change, the legacies of colonialism, and possible futures".[73] In this light, the right to be cold can be understood not as a demand the law must finally answer, but as an invitation the law is only beginning to hear, an invitation to inhabit uncertainty and to recognize, beneath the melting, a world capable of speech.

[72] Todd argues that Indigenous conceptions of land, water, animals, and ice are grounded in relations of kinship and reciprocity rather than ownership or management, such that ethical responsibility flows from ongoing social obligations to more-than-human relations rather than from regimes of preservation, control, or property. See Todd (2016), pp. 4–22.

[73] Riquet and Finbog (2023), p. 20.

References

Antoniazzi, Chiara Tea. 2024. Extraterritorial Human Rights Obligations in the Area of Climate Change: Why the European Union Should Take Them Seriously. *European Papers: A Journal on Law and Integration* 9 (2): 479–512.

Boetzkes, Amanda, and Jeff Diamanti. 2020. At the Moraine. *e-flux*. https://www.e-flux.com/architecture/accumulation/341644/at-the-moraine (accessed on 19th of February 2026).

Bosselmann, Klaus. 2017. *The Principle of Sustainability: Transforming Law and Governance*. 2nd ed. New York: Routledge.

Campt, Tina M. 2023. *A Black Gaze: Artists Changing How We See*. Cambridge, MA: The MIT Press.

Cruikshank, Julie. 2005. *Do Glaciers Listen? Local Knowledge, Colonial Encounters, and Social Imagination*. Vancouver: UBC Press.

Decision — Inter-American Commission on Human Rights: Petition Regarding Global Warming Caused by Acts and Omissions of the United States. *ClimateCaseChart*, https://admin.climatecasechart.com/wp-content/uploads/non-us-case-documents/2006/20061116_na_decision.pdf (accessed October 10, 2025).

Delgado, Richard. 1989. Storytelling for Oppositionists and Others. *Michigan Law Review* 87 (8): 2411–2441.

Dworkin, Ronald. 1986. *Law's Empire*. Cambridge, MA: Harvard University Press.

Fish, Stanley. 1982. Working on the Chain Gang: Interpretation in Law and Literature. *Texas Law Review* 60 (4): 551–567.

Gordon, Gwendolyn J. 2018. Environmental Personhood. *Columbia Journal of Environmental Law* 43 (1): 49–91.

Gremaud, Ann-Sofie N., and Kirsten Thisted. 2020. *Denmark and the New North Atlantic*. Aarhus: Aarhus University Press.

Hart, H. L. A. 1994. *The Concept of Law*. 2nd ed. Oxford: Oxford University Press.

Hiskes, Richard P. 2009. *The Human Right to a Green Future: Environmental Rights and Intergenerational Justice*. Cambridge: Cambridge University Press.

Jacobsen, Ushma Chauhan. 2022. The Entanglements of English in Contemporary Greenland. *Nordlit* 45 (1–2): 19–40.

Jodoin, Sébastien, et al. 2020. Realizing the Right to Be Cold? Framing Processes and Outcomes Associated with the Inuit Petition on Human Rights and Global Warming. *Law & Society Review* 54 (1): 168–200.

Kleemann, Jessie. 2021. *Arkhticós Dolorôs*. Copenhagen: Forlaget Arena.

Knox, John H. 2009. Linking Human Rights and Climate Change at the United Nations. *Harvard Environmental Law Review* 33:477–498.

Kotzé, Louis J. 2014. Rethinking Global Environmental Law and Governance in the Anthropocene. *Journal of Energy & Natural Resources Law* 32 (2): 121–156.

Kotzé, Louis J. 2020. Earth System Law: The Juridical Dimensions of the Anthropocene. *Transnational Environmental Law* 9 (3): 429–453.

Kuhlmann, Annelis. 2017. Strawberry Fields Not Forever: Iceberg Reflections on Performing Greenland. *Critical Stages* 30. https://www.critical-stages.org/30/strawberry-fields-not-forever-iceberg-reflections-on-performing-greenland/ (accessed on 19 March 2026).

Levit, Nancy. 1997. Listening to Tribal Stories. *Arizona Law Review* 39:389–416.

Limon, Marc. 2009. Human Rights and Climate Change: Constructing a Case for Political Action. *Harvard Environmental Law Review* 33 (2): 439–498.

Link, Beth, and Tyson E. Lewis. 2025. Toward an Ethic of Adjacency: Defining Critical, Arts-Based Phenomenological Breaching Experiments. *Qualitative Inquiry* 31 (1): 1–11.

Lopez, Barry. 1986. *Arctic Dreams: Imagination and Desire in a Northern Landscape*. New York: Scribner.

Norman, David W. 2022. Jessie Kleemann's Art of Survival. *Peripeti* 19 (37): 30–43.

Norman, David Winfield. 2018. En luktende diskurs: Jessie Kleemann og grønlandsk kunsthistorie mellom spekk og terpentin. *Kunst og Kultur* 101 (3): 149–165.
Pajević, Marko. 2020. Adventures in Language: Yoko Tawada's Exophonic Explorations of German. *Oxford German Studies* 48 (4): 494–504.
Paul, Katharina T., et al. 2022. Institutionalised Ignorance in Policy and Regulation. *Science as Culture* 31 (4): 419–432.
Pelizzon, Alessandro. 2019. *Ecological Jurisprudence*. Cham: Springer.
Peters, Julie Stone. 2005. Law, Literature, and the Vanishing Real: On the Future of an Illusion. *PMLA* 120 (2): 442–453.
Petition to the Inter-American Commission on Human Rights Seeking Relief from Violations Resulting from Global Warming Caused by Acts and Omissions of the United States. 2025. *ClimateCaseChart*, https://climatecasechart.com/wp-content/uploads/non-us-case-documents/2005/20051208_na_petition.pdf (accessed October 10, 2025).
Porter, Tenelle, et al. 2022. Predictors and Consequences of Intellectual Humility. *Nature Reviews Psychology* 1 (9): 524–536.
Reed, Hari, and Rebecca Hayes Laughton. 2023. Testimony on Whose Terms? The Cultural Politics of Forced Migration Testimony. In *The Palgrave Handbook of Testimony and Culture*, ed. Sue Jones and Richard Woods, 539–565. Cham: Palgrave Macmillan.
Report of the Office of the United Nations High Commissioner for Human Rights on the Relationship between Climate Change and Human Rights, UN Doc. A/HRC/10/61, January 15, 2009.
Riquet, Johannes, and Liisa-Rávná Finbog. 2023. Introduction: Mediated Arctic Geographies (at the Centre of the Map). In *The Mediated Arctic: Poetics and Politics of Contemporary Circumpolar Geographies*, ed. Johannes Riquet, 1–30. London: Routledge.
Tawada, Yoko. 2025. *Exophony: Voyages Outside the Mother Tongue*. Translated by Lisa Hofmann-Kuroda. New York: New Directions.
Thisted, Kirsten. 2017. Blubber Poetics: Emotional Economies and Post-Postcolonial Identities in Contemporary Greenlandic Literature and Art. In *Sámi Art and Aesthetics*, ed. Svein Aamold et al., 286–290. Aarhus: Aarhus University Press.
Thisted, Kirsten. 2025. Greenland: Indigeneity, Extractive Industries and State Formation. *The Global South* 17 (2): 166–176.
Todd, Zoe: "An Indigenous Feminist's Take on the Ontological Turn: 'Ontology' Is Just Another Word for Colonialism," *Journal of Historical Sociology* 29, no. 1 (2016): 4–22.
Watt-Cloutier, Sheila. 2015. *The Right to Be Cold: One Woman's Story of Protecting Her Culture, the Arctic, and the Whole Planet*. Minneapolis: University of Minnesota Press.
Wewerinke-Singh, Margaretha. 2019. *State Responsibility, Climate Change and Human Rights*. Oxford: Hart.
Weydt, Elisabet. 2023. *Die Natur hat Recht: Wenn Tiere, Wälder und Flüsse vor Gericht ziehen – für ein radikales Umdenken im Miteinander von Mensch und Natur*. Munich: Knesebeck.
White, James Boyd. 1973. *The Legal Imagination*. Chicago: University of Chicago Press.
Wright, Chantal. 2008. Writing in the 'Grey Zone': Exophonic Literature in Contemporary Germany. *GFL: German as a Foreign Language* 3:26–42.

Ecocide as Speech Act: How Anthropocene Narratives Perform New Crimes into Legal Thinkability

Amitabh Vikram Dwivedi

Abstract This chapter argues that 'ecocide' becomes legally imaginable not only through jurists and activists but through narrative acts that function like speech acts: texts *do* ecocide in language by naming a threshold of harm, assembling victims (often more-than-human or multi-generational), staging chains of culpability across corporations and states, and rehearsing juridical forms (indictments, testimony, tribunals, emergency norms). By treating key Anthropocene fictions as sites of proto-legal drafting, the chapter shows how narrative performativity expands the legal field: it reworks the grammar of responsibility (from isolated intent to distributed causation), stretches evidence beyond human witnessing (archives, sensors, ecosystems), and pushes jurisdiction beyond the nation-state (planetary commons, deep time). Literature does not merely 'reflect' environmental law's deficits; it supplies the scenes, voices, and procedural fantasies through which ecocide can be conceptualized as a crime that law could plausibly recognize, prove, and punish.

Keywords Ecocide · Speech-act theory · Performativity · Anthropocene literature · Law and literature

A. V. Dwivedi (✉)
Shri Mata Vaishno Devi University, Katra, India
e-mail: amitabh.vikram@smvdu.ac.in

A. Juster (ed.), *Legal Drafts in Anthropocene Literature*, SpringerBriefs in Law,
https://doi.org/10.1007/978-3-032-27283-6_6

1 Introduction

Ecocide—characterized as "extensive destruction, damage to or loss of ecosystem(s)"[1]—remains unsettled as positive law, particularly at the level of an autonomous international crime, even as scholarship and advocacy around its criminalization has expanded. While activists have pushed for its recognition for quite some time, as with Polly Higgins' campaign to make it an independent international crime, formal legal structures still favor anthropocentrism over the inherent worth of nature. This legal invisibility means that even the most severe anthropogenic harms are frequently treated as collateral damage or as ordinary negligence. Indeed, recent analyses note that, despite proposals since the 1970s, ecocide was largely absent from the post–Cold War discussions that shaped international criminal law and the formation of the International Criminal Court.

In the absence of formal crimes, "signals, narratives and performative moments"[2] regarding environmental catastrophe—from war-related ecosystem damage to the grand narrative of climate collapse—become crucial instruments of governance. By telling stories of disaster and implicating perpetrators, authors perform a significant symbolic function where "communicative and symbolic devices are explicitly recognized … as core instruments"[3] in aligning actor expectations. As Higgins argued, giving a name to massive destruction ("ecocide") is a fundamental act of "seeding intrinsic values";[4] such repetitive mobilization of symbols can provoke an experience that produces "therapeutic effects".[5] In this sense, the evocative narratives of the Anthropocene can make previously unthinkable crimes socially legible and legally significant.

The notion of ecocide is quickly moving from a tool of environmental activism into the orbit of formal legal debate, for one, it is at the advanced guard of this migration; it has defined the crime in its domestic code as "mass destruction of flora and fauna, poisoning of air or water resources, and also any other actions that may cause an environmental disaster".[6] By characterizing ecocide as the "emerging fifth international crime"[7] along with war crimes and genocide, that development declares environmental destruction can no longer be written off as collateral.

However, the regulatory law (and its jurisprudence) is already lagging behind the symbolic law because international architecture is "overwhelmingly anthropocentric in nature".[8] The existing mechanisms, such as Article 8(2)(b)(iv) of the Rome

[1] Mistura (2018), pp. 181–225, quoting Higgins (2012), pp. 62–63; cf. Mehta and Merz (2015), p. 3.

[2] Aykut et al. (2021), p. 524.

[3] Ibid., p. 521.

[4] Higgins (2012), pp. 9–10; Gillett (2022), pp. 348–350.

[5] Aykut et al. (2021), p. 532.

[6] European Law Institute (2023), p. 19.

[7] Kostin (2024).

[8] Gillett (2022), p. 6.

Statute, are critiqued for setting an "almost impossibly high damage threshold"[9] requiring that harm be cumulatively "widespread, long-term and severe" (International Criminal Court 1998) and that it qualifies only when committed during international armed conflict. As a result, international tribunals have generally neglected ecocide, leaving a gap where there is no existing law crafted around the "pervasive but elusive"[10] nature of dispersed long-term environmental damages.

Into that legal void, stories become crucial tools of governance. When the formal rules take time to emerge, signals, narratives and performative moments (as noted above) can align expectations among global actors and galvanize momentum for reform. By understanding law as a "narrative way of world-making"[11] it becomes possible for lawyers and activists to perform an important, symbolic work, rendering the "slow violence"[12] of environmental catastrophe visible and socially readable. By communicating through narratives that capture the imagination and ignite passion, writers bridge the gap between esoteric scientific knowledge and a shared moral imperative to demand accountability for what Said called the "normalized quiet of unseen power"[13] enabling ubiquitous environmental ruin.

Scholarship on environmental law and literature suggests that stories are constitutive of how we think about nature and justice. Michael Burger observes that environmental law is permeated by familiar tropes—including the wilderness, apocalypse, and toxic tales—and is made into "a kind of expressive, literary event"[14] as judges and lawyers draw on cultural narratives. Similarly, Chris Hilson argues that narrative "has an important role to play"[15] in enlivening environmental law and giving voice to the "marginalized (including, potentially, nature itself)"[16] who otherwise cannot speak.

In this sense, language about nature does not merely describe; it performs, as the "performative utterance"[17] attends to the "illocutionary force of the utterance"[18] rather than simple correspondence with facts. In this chapter, an 'ecocide speech act' is a narrative utterance (by a narrator, character, or institutional voice) that does more than represent ecological harm: it frames harm as a wrong that demands legal/moral adjudication and positions agents, victims, and forums in ways that resemble or prefigure legal reasoning. We treat an utterance as an ecocide speech act when it performs at least one of the following illocutionary functions, rather than merely describing damage.

---

[9] Killean and Short (2025), p. 4.

[10] Nixon (2011), p. 3.

[11] Hutchinson (1988), Dwelling on the Threshold, 14.

[12] Nixon (2011), p. 2.

[13] Said (2001), p. 10.

[14] Burger (2013), p. 1.

[15] Johnson (2015), p. 43.

[16] Hilson (2022), p. 2.

[17] Austin (1978), p. 6.

[18] Ibid.

Criteria

- Naming/Typing: labels the harm as ecocide (or frames it as a crime in equivalent terms) and stabilizes it as a recognizable category.
- Attribution: identifies who is responsible (a corporation, state, individual, or distributed network), not only what caused the harm.
- Victim-making/Standing: constructs an injured subject (people, ecosystems, future generations) as worthy of hearing, representation, or claim-making.
- Forum-building: stages or implies a scene of judgment (tribunal, hearing, investigation, evidence, indictment) or a procedural pathway that makes prosecution imaginable.
- Norm projection: signals a rule-like demand ("this should be punishable," "this must be judged") and invites moral or legal evaluation.
- Calling these moments "speech acts" is an analytic claim about what narrative language *does*—it does not presume that ecocide is already a settled offence in positive international law.

From the perspective of speech-act theory, an utterance that names a harm or victim can "do things and create reality,"[19] producing ontological effects[20] that work to bring certain kinds of realities into being. A story can thus enact an idea—for example, by declaring rights for future generations or creating an "embodied experience of the world as it could be"[21]—thereby helping to make novel legal norms conceivable.

This chapter explores how two works of climate fiction act as performative moments that perform the crime of ecocide into legal thinkability. It asks: what does it take to make "ecocide"—characterized as the "extensive destruction, damage to or loss of ecosystem(s)"[22]—an object of legal discourse? Fictional narratives provide a procedural imagination and victim archives which supply language, actors, and scenarios that stretch our sense of what can be prosecuted. In the Anthropocene—an age where "human influence has become so large"[23] that it acts as a geomorphic force[24]—literature has become a laboratory for rights and crimes. By examining Kim Stanley Robinson's *The Ministry for the Future*[25] and Indra Sinha's *Animal's*

[19] Cavanaugh (2015).

[20] Ontological effects are the widely accepted elements that come to feel like plain reality, what we often treat as 'naturalized assumptions'. When someone asks why things are a certain way, these assumptions are the ones that get defended with 'that's just the way it is'. The harder work in ontology is noticing these effects in the first place: recognizing which "givens" are not inevitable facts, but outcomes that have been made to seem self-evident.

[21] D'Souza and Staal (2022), pp. 34–43.

[22] Higgins (2012), p. 62.

[23] Biber (2017), p. 1.

[24] In 1873, when the Italian geologist Antonio Stoppani spoke about a "new telluric force which in power and universality may be compared to the greater forces of earth," referring to the "anthropozoic era"; cited in (Crutzen 2002, p. 23).

[25] Robinson (2020).

People,[26] we show how novels can summon new crimes into existence by naming and framing large-scale environmental harm. We pair these texts because they occupy contrasting but complementary narrative positions: Robinson offers institutional/procedural imagination (how an ecocide regime could function), while Sinha offers testimonial/victim archive (what such a regime must be able to hear and prove). Robinson's narrative envisions a body tasked with "defending all living creatures present and future who cannot speak for themselves",[27] while Sinha's "environmental picaresque"[28] humanizes the slow violence of "outsourced toxicity"[29] and the afterlives of industrial disaster. In so doing, they complement legal scholarship, such as Polly Higgins on "seeding intrinsic values",[30] and green criminology, which calls for a "named crime of ecocide"[31] within a "genocide-ecocide nexus".[32] Ultimately, we argue that narratives are not mere reflections but performances: they instantiate what Eric Biber identifies as pressures on a wide range of legal doctrines that will force law to change in the Anthropocene.[33]

Existing ecocide scholarship largely concentrates on definitional proposals, doctrinal pathways, and institutional feasibility, while environmental law-and-literature scholarship has tended to analyze how narrative represents ecological crisis. What remains underdeveloped is an account of how fiction can function as a jurisgenerative practice that performs ecocide into legal thinkability through identifiable narrative speech acts (naming, accusation, forum-building, victim-making). This chapter fills that gap by offering a criterion-based model of the 'ecocide speech act' and demonstrating its operation across two sharply contrasted Anthropocene novels.

2 Ecocide and Narrative: Preliminary Remarks

Research on ecocide, environmental crime, and the intersection of law and narrative spans several disciplines. In ecocide law, pioneering work—such as Richard Falk's 1973 proposal for an international convention and Polly Higgins' later campaigns—envisions a standalone international crime against nature, yet Branch and Minkova note that codifying such a crime has proved elusive.[34] Scholars have chronicled how earlier efforts to include ecocide in the Draft Code of Crimes against the Peace and Security of Mankind in the 1990s were unsuccessful, despite the concept "seeding

26 Sinha (2007).

27 Robinson (2020), p. 16.

28 Nixon (2011), p. 1.

29 Ibid., p. 5.

30 Higgins (2012), pp. 9–10.

31 Brisman and South (2019), p. 3.

32 Short (2016); Zimmerer (2004), pp. 49–76.

33 Cf. Biber (2017), p. 1.

34 Branch and Minkova (2023), pp. 51–79.

intrinsic values"[35] that prioritize nature's inherent worth over purely anthropocentric utility.

Though 'ecocide' is not yet codified as an autonomous core crime in international criminal law (for example, it is not currently a standalone offence within the Rome Statute). Concurrently, national legal systems are beginning to provide a category for such harm; for instance, Ukraine is "leading the charge"[36] by naming environmental warfare as ecocide under its domestic code (Article 441) and advocating for it as the "emerging fifth international crime".[37] Similarly, global justice scholars have proposed an international ecocide law to address the systematic destruction accompanying natural resource extraction, such as fossil fuel production and corporate pollution. These works emphasize that environmental damage poses an "existential threat to all life on the planet",[38] as ICC Prosecutor Karim Khan recently declared. Consequently, the criminalization of ecocide would require reconceiving agency beyond the individual,[39] potentially through expanded theories of organizational liability (often discussed under 'corporate criminal responsibility'[40] and/or doctrines of superior responsibility—pathways that remain legally uneven across jurisdictions and contested in international criminal law.

In current environmental criminal law, the prevailing approach is piecemeal, as formal legal systems frequently decontextualize principles of justice from their historical and sociological processes. Regulators may punish specific spills, illegal logging, or deforestation, but systemic devastation rarely fits neatly into traditional crimes because legal architecture often traces the "roots of the law and the concept of rights to the proprietarization of relationships",[41] turning rights into individual property and disrupting an awareness of our "inherent interdependency".[42] Numerous treaties, such as the Rome Statute's Article 8(2)(b)(iv), cover some destruction, but only in armed conflict and subject to a "military advantage" test regarding "widespread, long-term and severe damage" (Rome Statute 1998, art. 5.1). As Ukrainian prosecutor Kostin demonstrates, the targeting of dams or forests can be prosecuted as war crimes, yet peacetime industrial harm remains largely a regulatory issue often handled by fines.

Green criminologists critique this regulatory reliance, arguing that catastrophic events like Bhopal[43] or Deepwater Horizon are "crimes of the powerful"[44] that have more in common with mass atrocities than simple accidents. Commentators thus

---

[35] Higgins (2012), pp. 9–10.

[36] Kostin (2024).

[37] Ibid.

[38] Ibid.

[39] Higgins (2012), pp. 9–10.

[40] Cf. Schreurs (2020).

[41] D'Souza and Staal (2022).

[42] Ibid.

[43] Cf. Carrigan (2012), pp. 159–177.

[44] South (2014), p. 9.

call for the recognition of eco-crimes, noting that while the "full extent of ecocidal crimes exist in the future",[45] the fact that the "future has no jurisdiction"[46] requires a deterrent strike against these actions in the present. By highlighting systemic and transnational links, green criminology insists that ordinary categories of negligence are inadequate, asserting that the act of ecocide is a distinct crime rather than a mere health-and-safety violation.

The law-and-literature field demonstrates that "law always begins in story",[47] viewing legal systems not as mere static rules but as a narrative jurisprudence. Michael Burger's foundational research illustrates that legal battles are often driven by "competing narratives of nature and culture"[48]—such as the pastoral, the wilderness, or the apocalyptic—which judges absorb and retell, effectively making environmental law an "expressive, literary event".[49] Chris Hilson similarly notes that narrative has an important role in giving a "voice to the marginalized (including, potentially, nature itself)".[50]

This narrative jurisprudence highlights how legal storytelling is constitutive of identity, using characters, story events, and plots to drive a process of community- and identity-formation. From the perspective of speech-act theory, these narratives are not merely truth-evaluable statements but "performative utterances"[51] where "to say something is to do something".[52] Every turning point in a narrative functions as an "illocutionary act"[53]—an utterance that carries a certain force and can create reality or produce ontological effects.

Fictional storytelling acts as a laboratory to instantiate legal categories that do not yet exist, such as ecocide. By utilizing signals, narratives and performative moments, authors align expectations for a future legal order. This is exemplified by the "more-than-human tribunal"[54] envisioned by D'Souza and Staal, which uses "collective enactment" to "create an embodied experience of the world as it could be,"[55] replacing traditional rights with a notion of interdependency. In the Anthropocene, such literature performs a symbolic function that makes new crimes socially legible; for instance, Indra Sinha's narrator, Animal, makes a moral claim

[45] D'Souza and Staal (2022).

[46] D'Souza and Staal (2021), described as 'a more-than-human tribunal to prosecute intergenerational climate crimes'. The project draws conceptually on D'Souza (2018), and included testimony from collectives such as Kenya Land Alliance, Pueblos Indígenas Amazónicos Unidos en Defensa de sus Territorios, Vettiver Collective, and Synergie Nationale des Paysans et Riverains du Cameroun.

[47] White (1985), p. 168.

[48] Burger (2013), p. 1.

[49] Ibid.

[50] Hilson (2022), p. 2.

[51] Austin (1978), p. 58.

[52] Ibid. p. 6.

[53] Ibid., p. 109.

[54] D'Souza and Staal (2021).

[55] Ibid.

by recounting his history as a mystery defendant in the "Case against boy known as Animal".[56]

Finally, Anthropocene studies emphasize that our era requires new ontologies and ethics to navigate a world where human influence has become so large it acts as a geomorphic force that rivals the "greater forces of earth".[57] Philosophers and sociologists argue that this epoch must upend the Western dualisms and the human-environment binary that treat nature as "dead, inert particles"[58] or a passive resource to be managed at will. In legal terms, scholar Eric Biber predicts that these shifts will put "substantial pressures on the legal system, which will have to change in response".[59] New fields, such as Earth jurisprudence and the rights of nature, correspond with this shift, asserting the legal standing and legal personhood of rivers, forests, and future generations—a movement famously highlighted by Ecuador's constitutional recognition of "Pachamama".[60] Dipesh Chakrabarty argues that humanity must come to terms with this double view of itself as a modern individual and as part of a species within Earth's history. Fictional narratives operate as laboratories for these new rights; for example, in Kim Stanley Robinson's *The Ministry for the Future*, a body is created with a mandate to "defend[ing] all living creatures present and future who cannot speak for themselves".[61] Through fiction, "more-than-human tribunal" can be held, replacing conventional property rights with a "notion of interdependency", thereby making novel legal norms socially readable.[62] Such works facilitate a conceptual shift from an "anthropocentric frame" to an "eco-centric" one, challenging the logic of the "Plantationocene" and "Capitalocene" where "cheap nature is at an end".[63]

3 Theoretical Framework: Storytelling as a Performative and Ecological Act

This study draws on three bodies of theory. First, speech-act theory—pioneered by J. L. Austin and John Searle—teaches that "to say something is to do something".[64] Austin identifies "performative utterances"[65] as those in which the issuing of the utterance is the performing of an action rather than merely describing, reporting, or

56 Sinha (2007), p. 61.
57 Crutzen (2002), p. 23.
58 Merchant (1980), p. 193.
59 Biber (2017), p. 4.
60 Cf. Kaiser (2014).
61 Robinson (2020), p. 16.
62 D'Souza and Staal (2021).
63 Haraway (2015), p. 160.
64 Austin (1978), p. 6.
65 Ibid., p. 58.

stating a fact. In our context, asserting this is ecocide or they destroyed the Amazon is far more than a constative description; it is a performative speech act that frames an act as a crime and stakes a claim about reality, producing ontological effects or "naturalized assumptions of what constitutes reality".

As legal scholarship highlights, "performativity is the process of subject formation, which creates that which it purports to describe".[66] This process of subjection is vividly illustrated by the medical declaration "It's a girl!"[67] which constructs the subject's gender through the illocutionary force of the utterance rather than simple correspondence with pre-existing facts. Similarly, narrative can act as a narrative jurisprudence that creates new legal subjects—such as rivers, forests, and future generations—or new crimes by linguistic authority. We treat the naming of harm and victimhood in novels as a kind of illocutionary act that performs justice in an era of slow violence, thereby making ecocide—the "extensive destruction, damage to or loss of ecosystem(s)"[68]—a legible object of concern. Fictional narratives thus provide a procedural imagination that serves as a laboratory for rights and crimes in the Anthropocene.

Narrative jurisprudence and law-and-literature theories provide the conceptual glue for understanding how legal systems are not merely static rules, but a law as narrative practice. These narratives possess a specific form—utilizing characters, story events, and plots—to organize scattered facts into a meaningful moral drama. While stories in legal disputes are used to "persuade audiences to enact power in particular ways,"[69] fictional storytelling can propose a version of experience that envisions alternative laws and new legal categories. We are interested in how narrative structures operate as performative utterances that do not merely describe but create reality. For instance, in *Animal's People*, the narrator's evasive, humorous tone—declaring "I am a small person not even human"[70]—inverts the traditional victim narrative to subtly accuse the "Kampani"[71] of a crime where "now it's words that are choking us".[72]

In *The Ministry for the Future*, the formal reports and internal memos model a procedural imagination that, as with contemporary court records, is supposed to render the unthinkable legible. These are the tactics that produce legal effects, like the one challenged in the characterization of "Children of Kali"[73]—a "terrorist group"[74] from the present rulers' perspective vis-a-vis a "mass murderers"[75] under

---

[66] Beasley (2023), p. 1211.

[67] Ibid.

[68] Higgins (2012), p. 62.

[69] Cover (1983), pp. 4–10.

[70] Sinha (2007), p. 11.

[71] Ibid.

[72] Ibid.

[73] Robinson (2020), p. 49.

[74] Ibid., p. 97.

[75] Ibid., p. 99.

the purview of those evaluating from the "angle of the future".[76] This is analogous to what scholars of law and religion call *jurisgenesis*, in which communities go beyond state law to create their own norms. Both novels thereby radicalize insurgent legalities by way of counter-narratives, including reading vigilantism as a needful mode of planetary care committed to the defense "all living creatures present and future who cannot speak for themselves".[77] In this sense, the shared production of normative orders is a law that is in constant tension with sovereign power.

We situate these frameworks within an Anthropocene ontology, an epoch defined by a "human imprint on the global environment" that has become so large it "rivals some of the great forces of Nature".[78] This era necessitates facing a "fundamental crisis of modernity"[79] that has historically relied on the "hyperseparation of humans"[80] from the living world. We assume that nature and society are deeply entangled, rejecting the separability position in favor of the "inseparability of humans from nature".[81] In this view, agency is fundamentally relational, where "ontologically heterogeneous partners"[82]—including humans, animals, the climate, and corporations—"become who and what they are"[83] through "intra-action".[84]

Consequently, legal subjectivity in these texts is dispersed: in *The Ministry for the Future*, Mary Murphy leads a body charged with "defending all living creatures present and future who cannot speak for themselves".[85] Similarly, in *Animal's People*, the narrator "Animal" serves as a "condensation of occluded transnational economic relations",[86] existing as a "beastly boy"[87] who is simultaneously an individual, a "somatized foreign burden"[88] and a corporate allegory. This approach builds on post-humanist thought, specifically Haraway's "sympoiesis"[89]—the recognition that "nothing makes itself"[90] and all worlding is a process of "making-with".[91] We acknowledge Latour's actor networks and the call for a zoecentric shift that decenters the single rational subject in favor of a "multispecies becoming-with".[92]

In practice, we pay attention to how narratives distribute agency, asking who speaks for the earth and how expert knowledge and evidence are selectively

[76] Ibid.

[77] Ibid., p. 16.

[78] Steffen et al. (2011), p. 842.

[79] Latour (2018), p. 44.

[80] Plumwood (2009), p. 116.

[81] Hamilton (2024), p. 30.

[82] Haraway (2016), pp. 12–13.

[83] Ibid.

[84] Ibid., p. 159.

[85] Robinson (2020), p. 16.

[86] Nixon (2011), p. 57.

[87] Ibid., p. 57.

[88] Ibid., p. 67.

[89] Silova (2021), p. 587.

[90] Ibid., p. 594.

[91] Haraway (2016), p. 58.

[92] Ibid., p. 63.

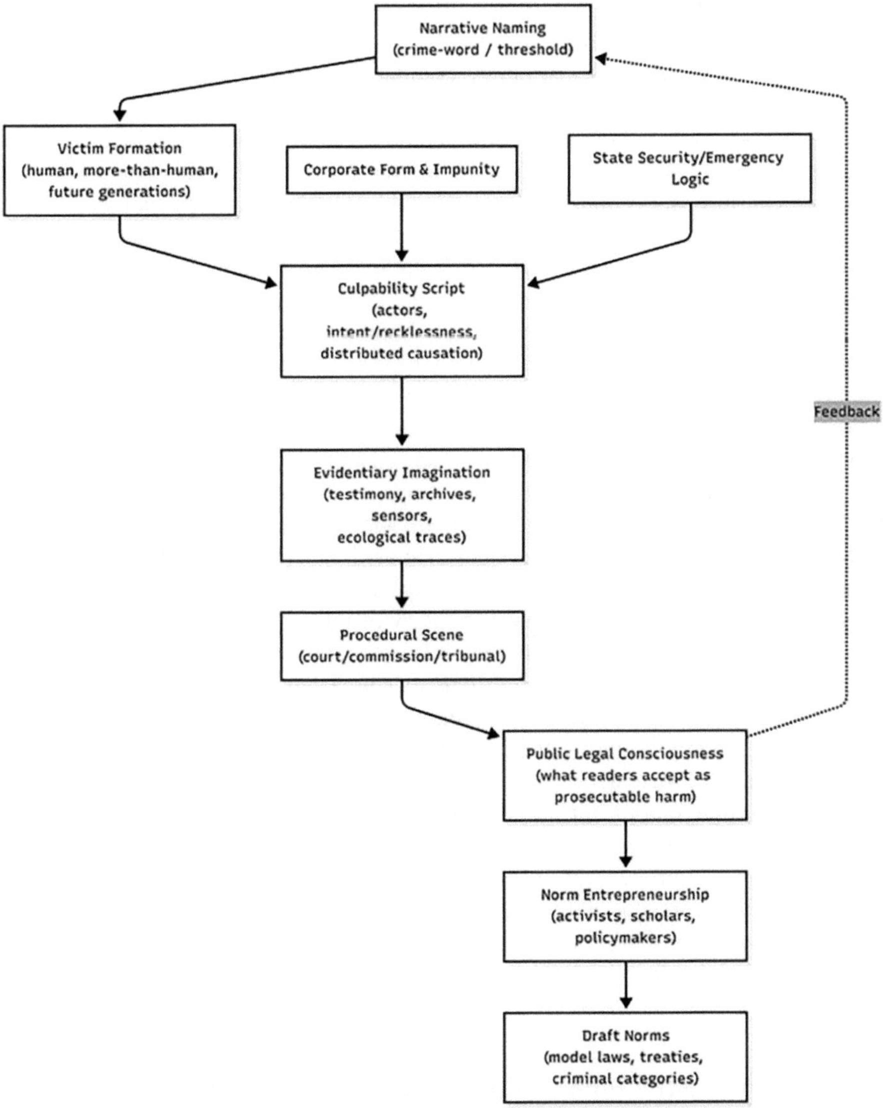

Fig. 1 Conceptual model of narrative speech-acts in ecocide discourse

constructed through climate data and testimonies. Character identities are thus shaped by ecological context, as "environment-related sources and causes of damage"[93] define the boundaries of their existence. In short, our theoretical lens sees storytelling as a performative and ecological act, a law as narrative practice. It is a speculative fabulation that braids possible paths and their ripple-effects into new, livable futures—and the ethical debts we must own to keep them alive (Fig. 1).

---

[93] South (2014), p. 12.

4 *The Ministry for the Future* and *Animal's People*

The analysis proceeds via qualitative, comparative close reading of two novels, supplemented by socio-legal discourse analysis. We treat each text as a "legal semiotic" object—a source of expressed law and policy imaginaries—and identify "ecocide speech acts" within it. These are moments where language in the fiction articulates harm, assigns blame, or even scripts judicial procedures. Our steps were: Perform detailed readings of *The Ministry for the Future* and *Animal's People*, annotating passages that name large-scale environmental damage or propose legal responses. By 'socio-legal discourse analysis' we mean a contextual reading of how the novels borrow, stage, and circulate legal language (rights, standing, jurisdiction, liability, evidentiary proof) and institutional genres (memos, reports, hearings, testimony), and how these textual moves echo or contest ongoing public and scholarly debates about ecocide, rights of nature, and corporate accountability. This is not an empirical study of courts; it is discourse-focused analysis of law as a cultural vocabulary and institutional imagination as it appears in narrative form. We draw on Hilson's and Burger's law-literature methods—looking at narrative structure, voice, and rhetorical tactics in relation to legal themes. Finally, in section 4 we will compare the two cases to see how each genre (global climate thriller vs. postcolonial tragedy) generates distinct yet complementary insights into the idea of ecocide.

Crucially, we focus on narrative *speech acts* rather than authorial intent. This means we cite what the novel's *characters or narrator* effectively say about law, rather than extrinsic social facts. However, we contextualize these within real-world debates (for example, relating the Ministry's proposals to actual policy proposals for central-bank climate action). In this way, we do not treat the novels as law, but as procedural imagination for law-making—akin to how Hilson sees narrative giving a voice to previously silent stakeholders.[94] Comparatively, we read *The Ministry for the Future* as a procedural–institutional genre experiment and *Animal's People* as testimonial–picaresque witnessing, asking how each generates distinct speech-act types (institution-building vs. accusation/testimony) that together make 'ecocide' legally thinkable.

4.1 The Ministry for the Future*: Procedural Imagination*

The *Ministry for the Future*, Kim Stanley Robinson's novel of a plausible and necessary world to come, is an uncanny project that lives somewhere between fiction and policy. Charged with representing future generations and protecting nonhuman

[94] Cf. Hilson (2022).

agents (e.g., animals, ecosystems), the Ministry fulfils a crucial symbolic role in the novel by recasting environmental harm as something more than collateral damage, but rather an offence punishable under international law. Under the leadership of Mary Murphy, a former union lawyer and Irish minister, the agency attempts to bridge the gap between weak international legal frameworks and the urgent requirements of a "planet in peril".[95]

As a testing ground for rights and crimes, the Ministry proceeds through an unprecedented series of mechanisms: (i) Legal Standing for the Voiceless: Within the novel's institutional design, the agency imagines standing on behalf of *autonochthoi* who cannot self-represent themselves—in echoing real-world earth jurisprudence and rights of nature movement. This is an effort to confer juridical significance on environmental injury, regardless of its impact on living persons. (ii) Technocratic and Artificial Intelligence Devices: The Ministry is a multidisciplinary group staffed with scientists, experts, and an AI tool like the character Janus Athena with which to sieve big data and construct a "workable shadow government"[96] or "Plan B"[97] in a world where the current economic system has failed. (iii) The Carbon Coin: In response to the tragedy of the time horizon encountered, when markets exclude long-term ecological costs, the Ministry advocates for a digital currency supported by central banks that rewards carbon sequestration; (iv) The Black Wing and Insurgent Legality: Acknowledging that international courts can be weak and lack a sheriff, what if there comes an underground bureaucratic unit within Ministry whose work is to cross all dubious lines with judicious violence necessary for change. This is a manifestation of the idea of insurgent legalities, in which collective ethics challenge formal law that fails to keep pace with environmental calamity. Robinson depicts the Ministry as an entity seeking to impose the "granite of the careening world"[98] to yield to the "gossamer"[99] of laws and treaties. In naming and framing ecological ruin as a crime with genocidal character, the novel functions as a performative narrative, stretching the limits of what is possible to think at law in the Anthropocene.

In the sources, *The Ministry* portrays an institutional design that legally treats the agency as having a form of universal jurisdiction to defend the interests of future generations and living creatures who cannot represent themselves. Although the Ministry is nominally a subsidiary of the Paris Climate Agreement and lacks a global sheriff to arrest offenders, it performs a powerful speech-act by creating a procedural forum where the crime of ecocide becomes legally thinkable and actionable.

---

95 Hamilton (2024), p. 69.

96 Robinson (2020), p. 358.

97 Ibid.

98 Ibid., p. 352.

99 Ibid.

The *Ministry's* quasi-jurisdictive function is made actual through a threefold strategy of evidence-gathering, financial architecture and crisis-mediation: (i) Legal Standing and Evidence: The legal department of the Ministry, represented notably by one Tatiana Voznesenskaya, is committed to the expansion of cosmic "circle of inclusion"[100]—thereby giving future people and ecosystems some juridical status. Drawing on empirical and case law, this effort relies on scientific, forensic, and economic analysis, such as the "Raftery modeling"[101] of temperature increases or blockchain transaction records, to bring cases against climate criminals in existing courts. (ii) Financial Leverage (Carboni): The novel undermines a legal and financial order by instituting the "carbon coin"[102] (or *carboni*). This currency, backed by a "Climate Coalition of Central Banks" (CCCB),[103] incentivizes decarbonization by paying for "carbon sequestration"[104] certified by Ministry teams. These plans are treated as plausible outcomes of concerted action when central banks, under the pressure of global strikes and financial collapse, agree to underwrite "hundred-year bonds"[105] and implement "carbon quantitative easing" (CQE).[106] (iii) Geoengineering and Mediation: The Ministry mediates crises by overseeing "geoengineering"[107] projects—rebranded as "Glacier Elevation Operations" or "GEO-BEGGING"[108]—such as pumping seawater onto the Antarctic ice cap or yellowing the Arctic Ocean to increase albedo. These are executed under international legal regimes governing the Earth system as a global commons;[109] and (iv) Subterranean Methods: Outside overt diplomatic circles, our story envisions a "secret division"[110] or "black wing"[111] engaged in illicit or undiplomatic action that targets, for example, coal plants. These insurgent legalities are portrayed as necessary to force the "granite of the careening world"[112] to yield when formal law fails to act with sufficient speed. The novel functions as a laboratory for "procedural imagination," showing how scoring and penalizing actors via a "global stocktake" can transition into a system of "biosphere and civilization health"[113] metrics.

[100] Ibid., p. 35.
[101] Ibid., p. 172.
[102] Ibid.
[103] Ibid., p. 342.
[104] Ibid., p. 420.
[105] Ibid., p. 173.
[106] Ibid., p. 174.
[107] Ibid., p. 265.
[108] Ibid.
[109] Ibid., p. 109.
[110] Ibid.
[111] Ibid.
[112] Ibid., p. 352.
[113] Ibid., p. 479.

In *The Ministry*, the narrative introduces a darker side of praxis through the creation of a secret "black wing"[114] within the titular UN agency. While the agency's leader, Mary Murphy, remains an institutionalist committed to the "rule of law,"[115] she eventually acknowledges that formal international courts are too weak and lack a sheriff to enforce climate justice. Consequently, she tacitly endorses an extralegal cell directed by her chief of staff, Badim Bahadur, which operates with "plausible deniability".[116]

This clandestine cell is closely tied to the *Children of Kali*, a radical group that identifies climate criminals—including weapons manufacturers and carbon-burning elites—as mass murderers when judged from the "angle of the future".[117] These militants carry out a "war for the Earth"[118] through diverse acts of violence, utilizing drone swarms to execute high-level executives in their homes and compounds, sinking oil tankers and container ships, and forcing coal plants offline through cyberattacks and physical destruction, and attacking financial distribution centers to drive down the stock prices of ecologically destructive corporations.

The novel reports these illegal actions in a matter-of-fact style, using chapters that read like news dispatches or clinical lists of targets followed by a repetitive boom. This stylistic choice performs an illocutionary act, blurring the distinction between crime and justice and forcing the reader to view violent eco-sabotage as a form of counter-jurisprudence. These militants act as agents of a counter-juridical ethics, asserting what scholars call "planetary sovereignty"[119]—a state of exception proclaimed in the name of preserving life on Earth beyond the limits of territorial state law.

In effect, the novel dramatizes Robert Cover's concept of "jurisgenesis," where communities create their own normative frameworks that exist in permanent tension with sovereign authority. By staging this dialogue between formal institutions and insurgent actors, Robinson instantiates the substantial pressures that the Anthropocene places on the legal system, suggesting that when the law is perceived as useless, society may inevitably move outside it to ensure planetary survival.

By envisioning an institutional design for the *Ministry for the Future*, Kim Stanley Robinson's narrative performs a range of speech acts that frame climate devastation as the overarching catastrophe of our era. The novel designates an international prosecutor-figure by establishing the Ministry as a subsidiary body of the Paris Agreement, explicitly charged with the identification and prosecution of

[114] Ibid., p. 99.

[115] Ibid., p. 415.

[116] Ibid., p. 110.

[117] Ibid., p. 99

[118] Ibid., p. 229.

[119] DeBoom (2021), p. 903.

climate and environmental criminals. It further outlines evidentiary and policy mechanisms—including "Raftery modeling"[120] of temperature rises, blockchain records of financial flows, and "carbon quantitative easing"[121]—as if they had already realized the legal and financial processes.

The novel challenges the piecemeal approach of existing law by dramatizing war-level destruction for which no traditional prosecutor can currently hold actors to account. For example, the devastation of millions in the opening heat wave is compared to the casualties of the First World War, with the narrative implicitly invoking terms like "mass murder" and "massacre". By providing a procedural imagination for a "more-than-human tribunal,"[122] the text creates a forum where ecocide becomes legally thinkable.

Furthermore, the novel performs the idea of climate murder by utilizing a cast list of victims and villains, such as the "Children of Kali"[123] who judge carbon-burning elites from the "angle of the future".[124] This framing aligns with the "genocide-ecocide nexus,"[125] which recognizes that destroying the "essential foundations of life"[126] constitutes a form of social death akin to recognized international atrocities. In short, the novel treats vast environmental harm as a crime that could, in principle, be policed and prosecuted, effectively moving it from a regulatory issue to a crime against peace.

Form matters here: Robinson's alternating modes (policy memo, report, list, quasi-journalistic dispatch) simulate the documentary genres through which international harms become legible as cases. These textual forms perform 'forum-building' speech acts: they stage evidentiary adequacy, bureaucratic authority, and procedural sequence (problem–proof–jurisdiction–remedy). The novel's genre-hybridity is therefore not decorative; it is the mechanism by which climate destruction is rendered prosecutable in the reader's imagination.

In *The Ministry for the Future*, Mary Murphy bumps against the hard ceiling of the possible: every treaty, bond, and back-channel remains structurally inadequate to the pace and scale of harm. The scene is a mirror held up to the present—international law with no global sheriff, courts that speak only when states feel like listening, and accountability forever deferred to the next summit, the next crisis, the next lifetime. Consequently, the narrative suggests that while "rule of law is all we've got,"[127] it is insufficient on its own to overcome the "tragedy of the time horizon" or the interests of "global capital".[128]

---

[120] Robinson (2020), p. 372.

[121] Ibid., p. 344.

[122] D'Souza and Staal (2021).

[123] Robinson (2020), p. 368.

[124] Ibid., p. 99.

[125] Short (2016); Zimmerer (2004), pp. 49–76.

[126] Ibid., pp. 836–837.

[127] Robinson (2020), p. 36.

[128] Ibid., p. 172.

Robinson deploys procedural imagination to simulate carbon politics at the global level via several non-standard means: (i) Economic Levers: The story is based on "carbon quantitative easing" and the "carbon coin,"[129] a digital currency printed by the Climate Coalition of Central Banks that they then showered on people who captured carbon sequestration. This creates a "carrot"[130] to balance the stick of carbon taxes, aiming to redirect global capital into "biosphere-sustaining actions".[131] (ii) Insurgent Legalities: The novel frames clandestine subversion—conducted by a "black wing" (TMF 451) of the Ministry and groups like the *Children of Kali*—as a necessary counter-jurisprudence. These acts of sabotage against carbon criminals (e.g., sinking oil tankers, destroying coal plants) are presented as a "War for the Earth"[132] designed to force the status quo to yield. (iii) Planetary Sovereignty: The climax envisions a world transformed by revolutionary pressure, including mass occupations of global capitals where citizens perform "alternative lifeways"[133] and demand that governments prioritize "biosphere and civilization health"[134] over profit; (iv) Shadow Governance: The narrative models "Plan B," an open-source "shadow government" and a new internet interface (YourLock) that allows for the creation of a "planetary civilization" grounded in "Gaia citizenship".[135]

Finally, the novel does not add to legal thought a statute on the books, but rather a conversation between official institutions and insurgent people. It suggests how these global accountabilities might work through a combination of legal reconstruction and communal normative production outside state law, both designed to confer legal standing on those unable to speak for themselves: future generations and ecosystems.

4.2 Animal's People*: Victim-Archive and Legal Refusal*

Indra Sinha's *Animal's People* (2007) is set in the fictional city of Khaufpur, twenty years after a catastrophic gas leak that serves as a direct stand-in for the Bhopal disaster. The novel is narrated through the subaltern voice of Animal, a young man whose spine was twisted by the poison of that night, forcing him to walk on all fours. Unlike the procedural and institutional focus of *The Ministry for the Future*, this work provides an intimate lens that archives the "slow violence" of

[129] Ibid.

[130] Ibid., p. 175.

[131] Ibid., p. 172.

[132] Ibid., p. 229.

[133] Ibid., p. 286.

[134] Ibid., p. 479.

[135] Ibid., p. 358.

environmental catastrophe—an attritional havoc that is typically "out of sight" and "dispersed across time and space".[136]

The narrative documents the daily life of disaster survivors under the shadow of corporate impunity, primarily embodied by the "Kampani."[137] The Kampani's bosses in "Amrika"[138] have spent decades evading the "Naya Adalat"[139] court, claiming it lacks jurisdiction, while the poisons continue to perform their industrious work in the communal bloodstream and the city's aquifers. Animal's physical form acts as a "somatized foreign burden";[140] his bent posture is a physical condensation of occluded transnational economic relations, literally buckling under the weight of an unacknowledged colonial load.

In *Animal's People*, Indra Sinha constructs a narrative of legal refusal that exposes the formal legal system as a 'farce' incapable of addressing the "slow violence"[141] of industrial catastrophe. Animal, the narrator, explicitly scoffs at the vocabulary of the "Jarnalis" (journalist), asserting that while they both use words like "rights, law, justice," these terms "don't mean the same" in the mouth of a victim.[142] He relies on the activist Zafar's description of such legalisms as being like "shadows the moon makes in the Kampani's factory, always changing shape," concluding that while the disaster began with poison, it is now these empty words that are "choking us".[143] The novel punctures the illusion that formal charters or courts can save victims by documenting the eighteen-year failure of the "Naya Adalat"[144] (New Court) to bring the "Kampani" to account. The Kampani's bosses in "Amrika" simply refuse to appear, claiming the court has "no jurisdiction over them".[145]

The *Animal's People* functions as a performative speech-act of naming and testifying, where the act of telling his story "from the heart"[146] into a series of tapes performs the action of creating a subject that the legal world refuses to acknowledge. By documenting "that fucking night"[147] and its twenty-year aftermath, the novel disrupts the "collective amnesia"[148] of public memory by constructing an archive of slow violence—an attritional havoc that occurs "gradually and out of sight".[149] Through Animal's anecdotes, poetry, and collected stories, the narrative

---

[136] Nixon (2011), p. 2.
[137] Sinha (2007), p. 11.
[138] Ibid., p. 42.
[139] Ibid., p. 60.
[140] Nixon (2011), p. 67.
[141] Ibid., p. 2.
[142] Sinha (2007), p. 11.
[143] Ibid.
[144] Ibid., p. 60.
[145] Ibid., p. 62.
[146] Ibid., p. 220.
[147] Ibid., p. 13.
[148] DeBoom (2021), p. 900.
[149] Nixon (2011), p. 2.

preserves a visceral record of ecocide's consequences, specifically birth defects such as the "parapagus" child in a jar, poisoned land and water, and ruined livelihoods exemplified by survivors like Pyaré Bai.

This process represents a form of performative witnessing. Animal rejects being an extra in a foreign journalist's movie and instead addresses the reader directly as Eyes, asserting that "my job is to talk, yours is to listen".[150] While the formal *Naya Adalat* court is dismissed as a farce where the "Kampani" bosses never appear, the novel constructs a living courtroom of feeling and ethics. Through grotesque humor and candid confessions regarding his own filth, Animal positions the reader as a juror over a reality where words are choking us as much as the original poison. In this way, the act of storytelling provides a crucial evidentiary function, where the narrative voice carries the weight of proof that a crime has been committed, even when the formal legal system lacks a sheriff to enforce accountability.

Animal's taped narration and direct second-person address ('Eyes') are formal techniques that convert readership into a quasi-juridical audience. The confessional, episodic picaresque structure produces a serial evidentiary logic: each vignette functions as an exhibit that accumulates causal inference (continuing harm, delayed adjudication, concealed knowledge). In speech-act terms, the voice does 'victim-making' and 'attribution' work simultaneously, creating a claim-bearing subject while indicting the Kampani and the institutions that enable its absence.

By granting narrative agency to a victim who has been physically and socially twisted by corporate negligence, Indra Sinha's *Animal's People* reshapes the discourse of environmental crime from a distant legal abstraction into a visceral, ongoing accusation. Animal positions himself as a picaresque sleuth—or as he calls it, "Jamispond"[151]—utilizing his unique physical perspective to navigate the crevices of Khaufpur where official eyes cannot reach. Operating as a spy for the activist Zafar, he uses his "eyes, nose, ears, [and] brain"[152] to uncover the ways the "Kampani" is structurally exonerated by a legal system it simply refuses to acknowledge.

The novel functions as an underground archive, exposing crimes that are often shielded by the farce of formal proceedings: (i) Exposure of Trade Secrets: Animal reveals the human cost of the Kampani's refusal to share medical data, noting that while they hide behind trade secrets, the people are "choking" on the very words meant to deliver justice. (ii) The "Second Disaster": The narrative documents what scholarship calls a second disaster—the eighteen-year cycle of legal delay and neglect. This slow violence is seen in the abandoned factory where "wonderful poisons" continue their work in the aquifers, a crime for which the "Amrikan" bosses claim the court has no jurisdiction. (iii) Speech-Acts of Accusation: Each disclosed fact in Animal's tapes—from the contaminated well water to the government's

150 Sinha (2007), p. 22.

151 Ibid., p. 119.

152 Ibid., p. 35.

complicity in stopping medical relief—performs a performative speech-act that puts the reader in the role of the juror.

By using the novel form, Sinha says what the *Naya Adalat* (New Court) cannot: that conventional justice is "not up to the task"[153] of confronting a multinational entity that has effectively run away scot-free. The narrative insists that the legal system is often just a shadow the moon makes, shifting shape to avoid pinning down the powerful. In the end, the novel tears the victim-label off like a faulty gas mask and proclaims a "planetary sovereignty"[154] where the people of the "Apokalis"[155] author their own oxygen-rules, their own ethics of breathing, healing, and staying alive.

Indra Sinha's *Animal's People* archives an alternate justice by documenting the slow violence that is typically "out of sight" and resistant to traditional "dramatic packaging".[156] This justice is rooted in communal solidarity and the lived experience of the "people of the Apokalis,"[157] who find the formal legal system to be a farce. Animal spits on the holy trinity of "rights, law, justice," viewing these terms as "shadows the moon makes" that tighten around victims' throats while the Kampani keeps its hands clean and its ledgers open.[158]

The storytelling itself acts as a form of refusal; by recording his truth onto tapes for a "Jarnalis," Animal centers the unanswered cries of the poisoned. This act counters epistemic violence, ensuring that the survivors' stories count even when they are dismissed by official scientific or legal experts. The narrative deliberately withholds a success story, documenting instead twenty years of legal delay and neglect and a second disaster of corporate and governmental indifference.

The novel reaches its climax not with a legal adjudication, but with tragedy and revolution: the long-awaited hearing is postponed, triggering a violent surge into the factory and the eventual death of the activist leader Zafar. Even the collapse of the Kampani's secret deal is achieved through subterfuge—a stink bomb—rather than a final court verdict. By ending with Animal choosing to live "alone and free as an animal,"[159] the text amplifies moral accountability by refusing to provide the closure of a settled case. Ultimately, naming what happened and documenting the human toll—from the "death by indirection"[160] of the initial leak to the "monstrous intimacy"[161] of intergenerational mutation—is portrayed as the necessary precondition for any future reckoning.

---

[153] Ibid., p. 195.

[154] DeBoom (2021), p. 903.

[155] Sinha (2007), p. 9.

[156] Nixon (2011), p. 200.

[157] Sinha (2007), p. 9.

[158] Ibid., p. 11.

[159] Ibid., p. 380.

[160] Carson (1962/1992), p. 32.

[161] Sharpe (2009).

5 Comparative Synthesis

Kim Stanley Robinson's *The Ministry for the Future* pushes the boundaries of institutional canvas by imagining an entire legal-political superstructure established as a sibling organization to the Paris Climate Agreement. Specifically, the Ministry enacts a speech-act of design by establishing a space for the adjudication of ecocide, in which members of future generations and non-human agents become correspondingly legible. This imagined framework integrates environmental goals with novel financial mechanisms, such as a "carbon coin" digital currency and "carbon quantitative easing," both of which are treated as plausible outcomes of concerted central bank coordination.[162] The narrative marshals advanced evidence-gathering tools, including AI management of big data and scientific attribution modeling, to identify and penalize climate criminals globally.

However, while this is optimistic about nature's capacity to be regulated, the book accepts that formal law is often insufficient because international courts are too weak—there is no enforcement sheriff. As a result, the story presents an extralegal "black wing"[163] that commits acts of sabotage and assassination against parties who persist in burning carbon, depicting these extralegal actions as providing a needed counter-jurisprudence to the global state of emergency. This contrasts with the intimate lens of Indra Sinha's *Animal's People*, which archives the "slow violence"[164] of corporate impunity where the legal system is dismissed by victims as a shape-shifting farce. Ultimately, Robinson's novel uses procedural imagination to bridge the gap between weak existing treaties and the urgent requirements of biosphere health, even if it requires flouting legal norms to force transformation.

Indra Sinha's *Animal's People* contributes to the moral and testimonial terrain of ecocide by archiving the "slow violence"[165] of environmental catastrophe—an attritional havoc that occurs gradually, out of sight, and is typically not recognized as violence at all. By chronicling the lived experience of Animal, a young man whose spine was twisted by the poison of the Khaufpur gas leak, the novel provides depth on why ecocide is a distinct crime by making the harm visceral and somatized. Animal's body acts as a physical condensation of occluded transnational economic relations, literally buckling under the weight of a foreign burden that the legal system refuses to acknowledge.

The novel's first-person narrative and its status as an "environmental picaresque"[166] utilize literary hybrids—mixing gritty realism with elements of fable and subaltern literature—to mobilize empathy and sense-making. For example, the narrative includes hallucinatory sequences, such as Animal's conversations with a fetus in a jar, and the eccentric babble of Ma Franci, which collectively challenge the "visual

---

[162] Robinson (2020), p. 17.

[163] Ibid., p. 451.

[164] Nixon (2011), p. 2.

[165] Ibid.

[166] Ibid., p. 1.

orthodoxies"[167] of spectacular disasters. This framing makes ecocide thinkable by giving it a human face, centering the intergenerational harm where casualties are "postponed, often for generations,"[168] and poisons continue to perform their industrious work in the communal bloodstream and aquifers.

Together, the novels open complementary vistas. *Ministry* maps out *structures* for a future ecocide regime; *Animal's People* fills in the *content* of what such a regime would need to address. In the Ministry, green policy initiatives and climatologists form the protagonists, whereas *Animal* centers the marginalized victims. One imagines courts and treaties; the other imagines conscience and storytelling. Both, however, enact speech acts that link ecological harm to justice claims. Notably, each text unsettles conventional binaries: legal/illegal, act/victim, human/nature. Robinson's narrative destabilizes legal/illegal by framing sabotage as preservation,[169] Sinha blurs human/animal by making a "boy" literally an animal, yet fully human in his demands. These narrative moves expand the *terrain of political imagination*,[170] suggesting that what counts as crime is not fixed but open to new interpretations in the Anthropocene.

Table 1 Narrative elements and their performative legal effects in the two novels

Narrative feature	Performative effect (speech-act)	Implication for ecocide law
Naming of crime ('ecocide'/'madness of the Commons')	Declares an act as criminal and frames ecosystem harm as an intentional wrong	Makes ecocide thinkable as a legal violation and stabilizes it as a category of international crime
Institutional protagonist (the Ministry, etc.)	Enacts an arbiter or proto-prosecutorial figure; assigns authority to future generations	Suggests jurisdictional models such as a UN subsidiary body or international tribunal and possible enforcement mechanisms
Victim voice (Animal's memoir, testimonial narration)	Enacts witnessing and testimony; personalizes diffuse and abstract harm	Legitimates legal claims by evidencing injury and supports doctrines such as continuing harm or continuing tort
Radical action (Children of Kali, mass protests)	Reframes illegal acts as moral interventions; recodes 'terrorism' as ecological care	Challenges the legitimacy of existing legal orders and illustrates possibilities of insurgent or jurisgenerative law
Scientific discourse (climate data, modelling, statistics)	Mobilizes facts to support normative claims; renders harm measurable and legible	Grounds potential prosecutions in evidentiary standards, modelling causation and scale for ecocide claims

167 Ibid., p. 6.

168 Ibid., p. 3.

169 Cf. Amirouche and Bekkai (2025), pp. 53–66.

170 Ibid.

A summarized view of their comparative contributions is given in Table 1 and bullet points:

(i) ***Ministry for the Future***: *Strengths:* Institutional vision (UN agency; legal-economic tools), integration of climate science into law (attribution methods), portrayal of global cooperation. *Limitations:* Relies on extralegal violence and mass mobilization; does not yield a concrete legal verdict; assumes state actors have will.

(ii) ***Animal's People***: *Strengths:* Strengths: It gives the silenced a face, turns slow violence into durable testimony, indicts corporate impunity, and stirs the moral momentum law sometimes needs. *Limitations*: It stops at the courthouse steps—no draft clause, no statutory scaffold—content to chant rather than codify, to decorate justice rather than redesign it.

6 Conclusion

The study of these novels shows that literature can actively shape legal debates on ecocide. By staging hypothetical trials, new rights, and voices for the voiceless, narratives *narrativize law*. They open space for legal innovation: for example, by treating climate destruction as deserving punishment, Robinson's story invites jurists to consider redrafting offense definitions. By insisting on the ongoing suffering caused by ecocide, Sinha's story presses law to account for it. At a minimum, literature draws attention to the "existential threat" posed by environmental damage.[171]

If ecocide is ever to become a crime, it will probably happen thanks to a mixture of passion in the political sphere and cultural change. The former and latter overlap, with narratives helping enable the latter to become possible, as ecocide can be thought of as a crime. They build a discursive reserve of images and terms that lawyers and activists can tap into. Higgins, for example, discovered that focusing on nature as "intrinsically valued" subtly changes consciousness toward seeing ecocide.[172] They are what literature does too: by giving ecosystems, and even future generations of people, narrative presence, they contribute to the collective feeling that destroying nature is something for which you can be held accountable. Similarly, Burger and Hilson argue that intra-textual narrative instructs judges and legislators to consider ethically relevant interests beyond the narrow concerns of litigant citizens.[173]

Ultimately, writing fiction about ecocide is a kind of law-making from below: it performs the speech-act of outlawry before the law actually does. As Haraway puts it (via Robinson's response), such speculative fabulations do not prescribe policy but "expand the horizon of the imaginable." In other words, *the Ministry for Future*

---

[171] Kostin (2024).

[172] Higgins, "Seeding Intrinsic Values," 10. (2012).

[173] Kuh (2020); Biber (2022), pp. 1–24.

and *Animal's People* do not legislate ecocide; they legitimate its conceptual existence. If modern law is to recognize ecocide, it will be because people can imagine it—and imagination is nurtured by narratives. As Higgins asserts, "seeds of law" are planted once a phenomenon is named and discussed publicly.[174]

In conclusion, literature contributes critically to legal debates by linking storytelling with rights. It insists that "the environment" is not a silent backdrop but a "victim" with a story to tell.[175] These novelistic "speech acts" thus suggest new categories—ecocide, climate genocide, hydro-terrorism—that may one day enter statutes. They also underline the failures of existing law, spurring reform. As the ICC explores environmental accountability, and as more countries adopt ecocide provisions, the imaginative groundwork laid by such narratives will become increasingly relevant. Perhaps in future courts and parliaments, prosecutors and judges will recall these speculative visions. Until then, the task of literature is to keep speaking for the Earth; for as Robinson's narrator reminds us, we owe it not only to "everyone she knew," but to all tangled life, to "keep going" and voice these crimes.[176]

References

Amirouche, Nassima, and Selma Bekkai. 2025. Green Fury or Chaos? Understanding Ecoterrorism through Kim Stanley Robinson's *Ministry for the Future*. In *Aleph*, 5 January 2025, 53–66. https://aleph.edinum.org/14431 (accessed on 7 January 2026).

Austin, J. L. 1978. In *How to Do Things with Words*, ed. J. O. Urmson and Marina Sbisà, 2nd ed. Cambridge, MA: Harvard University Press.

Aykut, Stefan C., et al. 2021. 'Incantatory' Governance: Global Climate Politics' Performative Turn and Its Wider Significance for Global Politics. *International Politics* 58:519–540.

Beasley, M. B. 2023. How to (Not) Do Things with Judicial Opinions: Minding the Performative Power of Facts and Dicta. *University of Colorado Law Review* 94:1199–1256.

Biber, Eric. 2017. Law in the Anthropocene Epoch. *Georgetown Law Journal* 106 (1): 1–68.

Biber, Eric. 2022. Law in the Anthropocene Epoch: An Introduction. *Journal of Environmental Law* 34 (1): 1–24. https://doi.org/10.1093/jel/eqab043 (accessed on 27 December 2025).

Branch, Adam, and Liana Minkova. 2023. Ecocide, the Anthropocene, and the International Criminal Court. *Ethics & International Affairs* 37 (1): 51–79. https://doi.org/10.1017/S0892679423000059 (accessed on 1 January 2026).

Brisman, Avi, and Nigel South. 2019. Green Criminology and Environmental Crimes and Harms. *Sociology Compass* 13 (1): 1–12. https://doi.org/10.1111/soc4.12650 (accessed on 28 December 2025).

Burger, Michael. 2013. Environmental Law/Environmental Literature. *Ecology Law Quarterly* 40 (1): 1–44.

Carrigan, Anthony. 2012. 'Justice Is on Our Side'? *Animal's People*, Generic Hybridity, and Eco-Crime. *Journal of Commonwealth Literature* 47 (2): 159–177.

Carson, Rachel. 1992/1962. *Silent Spring*. Boston: Houghton Mifflin.

---

[174] Crutzen and Stoermer (2010).

[175] Kostin (2024); Sinha (2024), pp. 1–13.

[176] Sethness Castro (2021).

Cavanaugh, Jillian R. 2015. Performativity. In *Oxford Bibliographies in Anthropology*. Oxford University Press. https://www.oxfordbibliographies.com/abstract/document/obo-9780199766567/obo-9780199766567-0114.xml (accessed on 5 January 2026).

Cover, Robert M. 1983. Foreword: Nomos and Narrative. *Harvard Law Review* 97 (1): 4–68.

Crutzen, Paul J. 2002. Geology of Mankind. *Nature* 415 (23). https://doi.org/10.1038/415023a (accessed on 31 December 2025).

D'Souza, Radha. 2018. *What's Wrong with Rights? Social Movements, Law and Liberal Imaginations*. London: Pluto Press.

D'Souza, Radha, and Jonas Staal. 2021. *Court for Intergenerational Climate Crimes (CICC)*, staged at Framer Framed, Amsterdam, 28–31 October 2021.

D'Souza, Radha, and Jonas Staal. 2022. "Indicting the Poisonous Imaginary", interview by Stephanie Bailey. *Art Papers* 45 (3): 34–43. https://www.artpapers.org/indicting-the-poisonous-imaginary-radha-dsouza-and-jonas-staal/ (accessed on 7 January 2026).

DeBoom, Meredith J. 2021. Climate Necropolitics: Ecological Civilization and the Distributive Geographies of Extractive Violence in the Anthropocene. *Annals of the American Association of Geographers* 111 (3): 900–912. https://doi.org/10.1080/24694452.2020.1843995 (accessed on 3 January 2026).

European Law Institute. 2023. *ELI Report on Ecocide: Model Rules for an EU Directive and a Council Decision*. Vienna: European Law Institute.

Gillett, Matthew. 2022. *Prosecuting Environmental Harm before the International Criminal Court*. Cambridge, UK: Cambridge University Press.

Hamilton, Rebecca. 2024. Criminalizing Ecocide. In American University Washington College of Law, Faculty Scholarship, 2024. https://digitalcommons.wcl.american.edu/facsch_law-rev/2247 (accessed on 6 January 2026).

Haraway, Donna. 2016. *Staying with the Trouble: Making Kin in the Chthulucene*. Durham, NC: Duke University Press.

Haraway, Donna J. 2015. Anthropocene, Capitalocene, Plantationocene, Chthulucene: Making Kin. *Environmental Humanities* 6 (1): 159–165.

Higgins, Polly. 2012. Seeding Intrinsic Values: How a Law of Ecocide Will Shift Our Consciousness. *Cadmus* 1 (5): 9–10.

Hilson, Chris. 2022. The Role of Narrative in Environmental Law: The Nature of Tales and Tales of Nature. *Journal of Environmental Law* 34 (1): 1–22. https://doi.org/10.1093/jel/eqab043 (accessed on 27 December 2025).

Hutchinson, Allan C. 1988. Dwelling on the Threshold: Critical Essays on Modern Legal Thought . Toronto: Carswell.

Johnson, Casey Rebecca. 2015. Speech Acts and Silencing: A Social Account of Speech Action and Restrictions on Speech. In PhD diss., University of Connecticut.

Kaiser, Anna. 2014. *Who Is Marching for Pachamama? An Intersectional Analysis of Environmental Struggles in Bolivia under the Government of Evo Morales*. In PhD diss., Faculty of Social Sciences, Lund University.

Killean, Rachel, and Damien Short. 2025. A Critical Defence of the Crime of Ecocide. *Environmental Politics*1–21. https://doi.org/10.1080/09644016.2025.2492441 (accessed on 30 December 2025).

Kostin, Andriy. 2024. Ecocide as a Weapon of War. In *International Bar Association (Global Insight)*, 21 May 2024. https://www.ibanet.org/Ecocide-as-a-weapon-of-war (accessed on 26 December 2025).

Kuh, Katrina Fischer. 2020. *Narratives of Nature and Culture in U.S. Climate Litigation*. In Sabin Center for Climate Change Law Working Paper Series, New York: Columbia Law School. https://scholarship.law.columbia.edu/sabin_climate_change/8 (accessed on 28 December 2025).

Latour, Bruno. 2018. "Anthropocene Lecture: Bruno Latour", video, 44:37, Anthropocene Curriculum (YouTube), 4 May 2018. https://youtu.be/UtaEJo-jo8Q (accessed on 4 January 2026).

Mehta, Sailesh, and Prisca Merz. 2015. Ecocide—A New Crime Against Peace? *Environmental Law Review* 17 (1): 3–14.

Merchant, Carolyn. 1980. *The Death of Nature: Women, Ecology, and the Scientific Revolution*. New York: HarperCollins.

Mistura, Alessandra. 2018. Is There Space for Environmental Crimes Under International Criminal Law? The Impact of the Office of the Prosecutor Policy Paper on Case Selection and Prioritization on the Current Legal Framework. *Columbia Journal of Environmental Law* 43 (1): 181–225.

Nixon, Rob. 2011. *Slow Violence and the Environmentalism of the Poor*. Cambridge, MA: Harvard University Press.

Plumwood, Val. 2009. Nature in the Active Voice. *Australian Humanities Review* 46:113–129.

Robinson, Kim Stanley. 2020. *The Ministry for the Future*. New York: Orbit.

Said, Edward. 2001. The Public Role of Writers and Intellectuals. In *The Nation*, 17 September 2001, 19–39.

Schreurs, Fien. 2020. Revisiting the Possibility of Corporate Criminal Responsibility in International Criminal Law: Amending Article 25 of the Rome Statute to Include Legal Entities within the Jurisdiction of the ICC. In *research paper*, Faculty of Law, University of Ottawa, 15 August 2020. https://ssrn.com/abstract=3700432 (accessed on 4 January 2026).

Sethness Castro, Javier. 2021. Salvaging the Future: A Review of *The Ministry for the Future*. In *The Institute for Anarchist Studies*, 7 June 2021. https://anarchiststudies.org/salvaging-the-future/ (accessed on 29 December 2025).

Sharpe, Christina. 2009. *Monstrous Intimacies: Making Post-Slavery Subjects*. Durham, NC: Duke University Press.

Short, Damien. 2010. Cultural Genocide and Indigenous Peoples: A Sociological Approach. *The International Journal of Human Rights* 14 (6): 831–846.

Short, Damien. 2016. *Redefining Genocide: Settler Colonialism, Social Death, and Ecocide*. London: Zed Books.

Silova, Iveta. 2021. Facing the Anthropocene: Comparative Education as Sympoiesis. *Comparative Education Review* 65 (4): 587–616. https://doi.org/10.1086/716664 (accessed on 28 December 2025).

Sinha, Anoushka. 2024. Disabling/Debilitating Environment: A Biopolitical Reading of Indra Sinha's *Animal's People*. *Lapis Lazuli: An International Literary Journal* 14 (2): 1–13.

Sinha, Indra. 2007. *Animal's People*. New York: Simon & Schuster.

South, Nigel. 2014. Green Criminology: Reflections, Connections, Horizons. *International Journal for Crime, Justice and Social Democracy* 3:5–20.

Steffen, Will, Jacques Grinevald, Paul Crutzen, and John McNeill. 2011. The Anthropocene: Conceptual and Historical Perspectives. *Philosophical Transactions of the Royal Society A* 369 (1938): 842. https://doi.org/10.1098/rsta.2010.0327 (accessed on 24 December 2025).

White, James Boyd. 1985. *Heracles' Bow: Essays on the Rhetoric and Poetics of the Law*. Madison: University of Wisconsin Press.

Zimmerer, Jürgen. 2004. Colonialism and the Holocaust: Towards an Archeology of Genocide. In *Genocide and Settler Society: Frontier Violence and Stolen Indigenous Children in Australian History*, ed. A. Dirk Moses, 49–76. New York: Berghahn Books.

International Legal Texts

International Criminal Court. 2011. *Rome Statute of the International Criminal Court (consolidated text including 2010 amendments)*. The Hague: International Criminal Court. https://www.icc-cpi.int/publications/core-legal-texts/rome-statute-international-criminal-court (accessed on 6 January 2026).

Rome Statute of the International Criminal Court. 1998. *Rome Statute of the International Criminal Court*, 17 July 1998, 2187 U.N.T.S. 90.

MIX
Papier aus verantwortungsvollen Quellen
Paper from responsible sources
FSC® C105338

If you have any concerns about our products,
you can contact us on
ProductSafety@springernature.com

In case Publisher is established outside the EU,
the EU authorized representative is:
Springer Nature Customer Service Center GmbH
Europaplatz 3, 69115 Heidelberg, Germany

Printed by Libri Plureos GmbH
in Hamburg, Germany